Hiking the
Green Mountains

Hiking the
Green Mountains

A Guide to 35 of the Region's Best Hiking Adventures

Lisa Densmore

FALCON GUIDES ®

GUILFORD, CONNECTICUT
HELENA, MONTANA
AN IMPRINT OF THE GLOBE PEQUOT PRESS

To my son Parker, my favorite hiking pal, and to Bravo and Riot, my two Chesapeake Bay retrievers who have kept me company on many miles of trails in Vermont.

To buy books in quantity for corporate use or incentives, call **(800) 962–0973** or e-mail **premiums@GlobePequot.com.**

FALCONGUIDES®

Copyright © 2009 by Morris Book Publishing, LLC

Falcon, FalconGuides, and Outfit Your Mind are registered trademarks of Morris Book Publishing, LLC.

Interior photos © Lisa Densmore

Text design: Nancy Freeborn
Project Manager: Julie Marsh
Layout artist: Kevin Mak

Maps created by DesignMaps © Morris Book Publishing, LLC

Library of Congress Cataloging-in-Publication Data

Densmore, Lisa Feinberg.
 Hiking the Green Mountains : a guide to 35 of the region's best hiking adventures / Lisa Densmore.
     p. cm.
  Includes index.
  ISBN 978-0-7627-4522-7
 1. Hiking—Vermont—Green Mountains—Guidebooks.
 2. Backpacking—Vermont—Green Mountains—Guidebooks. 3. Green Mountains (Vt.)—Guidebooks. I. Title.
 GV199.42.V42G743 2009
 917.43–dc22

                            2009003197

Printed in the United States of America

10 9 8 7 6 5 4 3 2 1

Contents

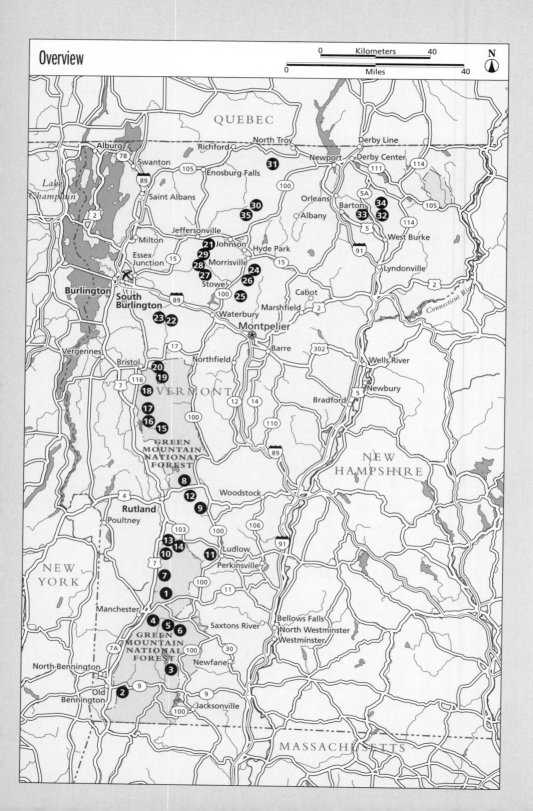

Acknowledgments

While this book bears my name as author, many have contributed to its pages in ways for which I am eternally grateful. First, I would like to thank Jason and Parker Densmore, not only for accompanying me periodically on the trail, but also for allowing me to escape into mountains to explore a number of routes for this book.

I owe a big thank-you to Pete Antos-Ketchum at the Green Mountain Club (GMC), for making sure that my prose is accurate. I am also eternally grateful to the GMC's trail crews, its summit caretakers, its "ridge runners," and its campsite caretakers. Without their efforts at keeping the trails and shelters in great shape, hiking in the Green Mountains would not be half as enjoyable or pristine.

I extend a similar thank-you to the USDA Green Mountain National Forest staff; the Vermont Department of Forests, Parks and Recreation staff; the Vermont Youth Conservation Corps; and the Westmore Association Trails Committee for their trail maintenance, education, and conservation efforts.

I am grateful to Peter Sachs at Lowa/XSocks and Gary Fleming at Lowe Alpine for supplying me with footwear, socks, and backpacks. My feet and my back could not have been happier on the trail.

I would also like to thank my close friend Jack Ballard. Though he has never hiked in Vermont, he probably feels he has been here after looking at countless photographs of mine while I worked on this book.

Finally, I would like to thank the many people who recommended or simply accompanied me on the routes in this book that I had never hiked before: Linda Barton, Gene and Woody Bergman, Mike and Kerri Bisner, Kate Carter, Jim Dooley, Jared Gange, Barbara Gerstner, Deborah Hannam, Whitney Hardeman, Edie Lodi, Peter Lodi, and Janne Piper. I appreciated your patience while I took field notes, your willingness to be models in my photographs, and most of all, your companionship on the trail. You made this project so enjoyable that it hardly seemed like work.

Introduction

Geology of the Green Mountains

The Green Mountains of Vermont are composed mainly of igneous granite and quartz, as well as metamorphic phyllite, schist, quartzite, greenstone, slate, and gneiss. The origin of the name "Green Mountains" is unclear, but one theory is because of the predominance of green-colored rock. The other theory is that the mountains are forested up to higher elevations than the neighboring Adirondacks to the west in New York and the White Mountains to the east in New Hampshire. About three-quarters of Vermont remains forested.

The basic topography was formed about 12,000 years ago when the last ice age receded. As the mile-deep ice retreated, it gouged the softer rock, creating the ledges and cliffs that provide many of the best hiking destinations today. A classic example is the sheer cliffs of Mount Pisgah over Lake Willoughby (see hike 32). The glaciers deposited large boulders, called *glacial erratics,* throughout the backcountry. They also left behind the scree and rocks that tumble down various Vermont hillsides, such as the boulder pile at White Rocks Ice Beds (see hike 14).

Flora

With their relatively low base elevations and exposed summits, the tallest peaks in the Green Mountains boast four different climate zones, each with distinct flora. Trailheads are typically below 2,000 feet in the zone called the eastern deciduous forest, made up primarily of sugar maple, beech, poplar, and yellow birch, or the mixed northern forest, which adds evergreens into the mix.

Wildflowers are plentiful from early spring through early fall. In the spring look for blooming trillium, bunchberry, and trout lily along the forest floor. During summer devil's paintbrush, violets, and various wild orchids

Vermont's state flower is the red clover.

1

give color to the woods and clearings. Early autumn's goldenrod, black-eyed Susans, and asters add to the vibrant fall foliage. Interestingly, the autumnal explosion of reds, oranges, and yellows is not due to an endemic strain of maple, but rather to the soil and climate. Red clover, Vermont's state flower, blooms from May through October. You'll also find a number of mushroom species growing on the forest floor and on tree trunks.

At 2,600 feet, trails begin to enter the boreal forest, which is mainly coniferous balsam fir, spruce, cedar, and hemlock. Species such as mountain ash and white (paper) birch also grow in the boreal zone. Flora in this zone can handle more extreme winter climates and are more exposed to biting wind, hoar frost, and fog.

Above 3,500 feet, trails pass through a subalpine zone called krummholz, which is composed of severely stunted, unevenly shaped trees that tend to grow with their "backs to the wind and their heads in the snow." With the extremely short growing season and severe weather conditions, many of these thigh-high shrubs are actually hundreds of years old. Wild blueberry, rhodera, and Labrador tea are also common in the subalpine zone.

Five of the peaks in the Green Mountains—Mount Mansfield, Mount Abraham, Lincoln Peak, Killington Peak, and Camel's Hump—have elevations over 4,000 feet. Three of these summits have a fragile alpine zone, which primarily supports low ground covers and lichens. Most alpine plants here are similar to those found thousands of miles to the north in the Arctic Circle, though they are genetically isolated and considered rare or endangered. The grasses that grow among the rocks in the alpine zone are actually rare sedges. In June and July, mountain sandwort, diapensia, and other delicate flowers add color and interest above tree line.

Fauna

Vermont has 42 species of reptiles and amphibians, 58 mammals, and 235 birds. Many are visible from the hiking trails if you are lucky. More likely, you will see animal tracks and scat. Whitetail deer and moose are the only wild ungulates in the state. Snowshoe hares, beavers, porcupines, red and gray squirrels, chipmunks, skunks, and raccoons are among the more common small mammals. You can hike in the Green Mountains for a lifetime and never see a catamount (mountain lion), bobcat, fisher, coyote, or fox, but they are in the woods as well.

Common birds along the trail include robins, tree swallows, black-capped chickadees, red-winged blackbirds, various woodpeckers, blue jays, ruffed grouse, and peregrine falcons. The Forest Service will close cliff areas to hikers if peregrines decide to nest there, so it is worth checking if you are planning a hike to a cliff-top destination from early May through mid-August.

The most dangerous creature in Vermont's backcountry is the black bear. In general, a bear will avoid hikers, but a hungry bear will raid a campsite if it smells food

◀ *Entering the alpine zone at the edge of the krummholz on Camel's Hump.*

(and their sense of smell is very keen). It will also defend a natural food source and its cubs. To minimize the chance of a bear encounter, do the following:

- Hike in a group during daylight hours.
- Make noise by talking or singing as you walk.
- Leave hair spray, cologne, scented soaps, and hand lotions at home.
- Never eat food or feed a dog in your tent.

Frog near Ritterbush Pond.

- Do not clean dishes within 100 feet of your campsite.

Always hang food, trash, and other scented items in a designated bear bag or bear-proof canister away from your shelter or campsite. The bag should be at least 12 feet off the ground and at least 8 feet away from the trunk of the tree.

Weather

Vermont has a temperate climate, with warm, humid summers and cold, snowy winters. The northeastern part of the state, called the "Northeast Kingdom," has exceptionally cold winters. The highest recorded temperature in the state was 105 degrees Fahrenheit in 1911. The record low was minus 50 degrees in 1933. The weather tends to present much greater hazards to hikers in the Green Mountains than wildlife.

The chart below gives average temperature by month in the state. Keep in mind that this is at the trailhead. Subtract 3 to 5 degrees for each 1,000 feet of elevation that you climb. For example, if it is 80 degrees at the base of Mount Mansfield, it might be 55 degrees at the summit, not including a stiff windchill.

Heat. July is particularly hot and humid, though June and August can have equally sticky days. Be sure to stay hydrated to avoid heat stroke. Experienced hikers sometimes bring a change of shirt to stay drier.

Vermont: Average Temperature High/Low by Month

Month	Jan	Feb	Mar	Apr	May	Jun	Jul	Aug	Sep	Oct	Nov	Dec
Norm High	25	31	43	51	64	76	81	78	71	54	36	28
Norm Low	4	10	22	30	43	55	60	57	50	33	15	7

Source: USTravelWeather.com

Hiker on the Long Trail to Sterling Pond in March. ▶

Lightning. If you are hiking and hear thunder, assume lightning too. At the slightest hint of a storm, head immediately below tree line to an area where the trees are at least twice as tall as you are. If this is impossible, try to find a low spot on the ridge where you can hunker down. Even below tree line, it is not safe to use a tree for shelter, especially a tall one. Find a depression in the ground and crouch down until the storm passes. If there are other people with you, spread out so that if lightning strikes, it does not hit everyone in your party.

Snow and ice. The average yearly snowfall in Vermont is 50 to 100 inches, but most of that blows off the tops of mountains and other areas of exposed rock. What's more, rock slab tends to freeze up before the rest of the trail. At the first signs of frost, it is a good idea to

A tree hit by lightning beside the trail.

bring traction aids, such as crampons and hiking poles, when you venture into the backcountry. Snowshoes are a must if the snow gets deep.

Once in a while, the Green Mountains get hit by ice storms rather than snow. Ice from these storms clings to trees, causing them to bend radically and sometimes break from the weight. Major ice storms can render hiking routes impassable due to tree damage. The same is true when a microburst hits. Though both of these types of storms are rare, they do happen. It can take trail crews many weeks to reopen a route due to the extensive damage done by these two natural phenomena.

Forests and Parks

Many of the trails in this book are located within the USDA Green Mountain National Forest. This 400,000-acre forest extends from the southern border of the state along the Green Mountains to Route 103, then from north of U.S. Highway 4 to just south of Waitsfield. Other trails, such as the Healdville Trail on Okemo Mountain (see hike 11), are located in state forests. Some of the trailheads, such as the start of the Sunset Ridge Trail on Mount Mansfield (see hike 28), are in state parks but the routes cross into state or national forest above the trailhead. Although the Appalachian Trail corridor is technically national park, none of the trails in this book traverse land that is managed as a national park. Two of the hikes, the White Rocks Cliffs and the White Rocks Ice Beds (see hikes 13 and 14), are in a designated National Scenic Area. These distinctions do not affect hikers, unless you have a dog. Leash laws vary depending on who manages the land.

Long Trail and Appalachian Trail

In 1910 the Green Mountain Club (GMC) established the Long Trail (LT), the first long-distance hiking trail in the United States. It was completed in 1930 and travels 272 miles along the high spine of the Green Mountains from the Massachusetts border to the Canadian border. Each year many "through-hikers" attempt to traverse the entire LT, though those in the southern half of Vermont might be attempting the 2,174-mile Appalachian National Scenic Trail (AT), which begins in Georgia and ends in Maine. The two trails coincide for about 100 miles in Vermont, from the Massachusetts border to just north of US 4 near Deer Leap Mountain (see hike 8). Both trails are marked with white blazes (a vertical rectangle painted on sturdy trees or bedrock). Side trails that lead to the AT/LT are marked by blue blazes.

Backpacking and Camping

The GMC maintains about seventy rustic cabins, shelters, and tent sites along Vermont's hiking trails. They are available on a first-come, first-served basis and typically sleep eight to ten people. If your party does not fill the cabin or shelter, please allow others to share the space with you.

In addition, the GMC and other trail maintenance groups have a number of tent platforms and primitive campsites scattered throughout the Green Mountains. During the summer and early fall, expect to pay a small nightly fee per person for the use of cabins, shelters, and designated campsites. Most shelters and campsites have a privy

Interior of Pico Shelter on Pico Peak.

(outhouse), a specific place to wash dishes, a fire pit, and a water source. Always filter water or use another water-purification method in the Green Mountains to avoid contracting the giardia parasite or other waterborne illness.

Some of the trailheads in this book are located in state parks with campsites that can accommodate car camping and RVs. Call ahead to be sure there is enough space, particularly during the summer and the fall foliage season (late September through mid-October). State campsites are closed during the winter and early spring.

Camping is also permitted elsewhere on public lands. Select a site that is below tree line and at least 150 feet away from trails and water sources. And try to find a site on a durable surface to minimize impact on the environment. Campfires are not recommended in the Vermont backcountry. Plan to cook over a portable camping stove.

Be Prepared: Backcountry Safety and Hazards

While the Green Mountains are relatively low compared to places like the Rockies or the Sierra Nevada, they are still mountains. As such, bad weather is foremost among the risks associated with hiking and backpacking here. The old saying "If you don't like the weather, wait a few moments" is often true. Regardless of the time of year, always bring layers of clothing, including a fleece or wool midlayer for warmth and a waterproof, breathable jacket to block wind and precipitation.

A typical muddy trail after a rainstorm.

Mud. Many trails are closed during the notorious Vermont mud season, which begins with snowmelt and ends by late May. But Vermont still averages 4 inches of rain per month in the summer, so mud is common on the trails here. Perennially muddy areas usually have narrow puncheon (split log) walkways across them to help keep your feet dry; otherwise, you will have to depend on your rock-hopping skills. Avoid walking off the trail to miss a mud puddle, which only widens the trail over time, contributes to erosion, and eventually leads to a costly trail relocation.

Brooks and streams. Streams are fickle in the Green

Poison ivy with its three leaves and red stems.

Mountains. They might be swollen and impassable during spring runoff or after a heavy rainstorm, and they might dry up completely by mid-August. Hiking poles can help you maintain your balance during a tricky stream crossing.

Bugs. Unfortunately, the Green Mountains are home to black flies, mosquitoes, and other pesky insects, such as deer ticks that might carry Lyme disease. Bug spray with at least 20 percent deet is a must during the spring and the summer months on the hiking trail. Wearing a ball cap or a wide-brimmed hat also helps.

Poison plants. There are only two poison plants in Vermont: poison sumac and poison ivy. You are unlikely to find poison sumac along a hiking trail because it prefers low-lying wet soil. Poison ivy, however, is common below 2,000 feet. Its usual form is a ground cover or low shrub, but it can also wind its way up tree trunks as a vine. Mature poison ivy vines become woody, resembling their host trees. Poison ivy leaves appear in clusters of three. Young leaves have a shiny olive hue, with hints of red. During the summer the leaves are true green, and in the fall they often turn bright red or red and yellow. Skin contact with any part of the poison ivy plant, dead or alive, will likely result in an itchy red rash. The rash is actually caused by urushiol oil and can appear anywhere from a few hours to several days later. If you suspect that you came

Stay on the trail so you don't trample fragile plants.

in contact with poison ivy, wash the area with soap and water as soon as possible to remove the oil. Depending on how sensitive you are, you have up to two hours to avoid the rash by thoroughly washing the exposed area.

Hunting Seasons

There are several hunting seasons in Vermont. The dates change annually, but in general, bear season begins around September 1 and runs through mid-November. Other big-game seasons (deer, moose) usually begin around November 1. Most hunters avoid popular hiking corridors, but it is always better to err on the side of safety. If you are planning to hike during hunting season, it is smart to wear a blaze-orange hat, jacket, and/or vest. Bright red is less effective if the leaves are still on the trees because the leaves are also red, though anything colorful is better than browns and blacks.

Zero Impact

It is every hiker's responsibility to help keep the backcountry as pristine as possible so that future generations can have the same enjoyable experiences. Here are several additional things that you can do to help:

- Limit the number in your party to eight or fewer.
- Avoid using soaps within 150 yards of water sources.
- Either bury or pack out human and dog waste.
- Carry out what you carry in.
- Leave plants and wildlife alone.

Hiking with Dogs

Every hike in this book has a notation about whether a hike is dog friendly or not. In the Green Mountains, the things that make a route difficult or impossible for dogs are ladders up rock walls, rock chimneys without ladders, and terrain that requires rock hopping from boulder to boulder.

Many fabulous dog-friendly hikes in Vermont end at an old fire tower. Please avoid taking a dog up a fire tower! Dogs find the geometry and scaffolding confusing. For Fido's safety and yours, please leave your dog below on a lead. He could care less about the view, but he might want to follow you up the tower's steep, narrow steps.

Some trailheads are located in state parks, which require dogs to be on leashes of 10 feet or less. You might have to show proof of rabies vaccine to enter a state park with a dog. Dogs should also be kept on a leash and on the trail in the alpine zone. After that, it's up to you, though other hikers appreciate when dogs are kept under control.

How to Use This Guide

The trails in this guidebook were selected primarily because they are all truly interesting, scenic hikes. They are spread geographically from the south end of the state to the north end to allow a number of options regardless of location. In addition, the routes vary by mileage and vertical rise. To find the best route near you, start with the fitness level of the weakest person in your party, then pick a hike length that is half what he or she is comfortable walking on a flat, paved sidewalk. For example, if you feel you can handle 4.0 miles in town, start with a hike that is 2.0 miles or less and then build up from there.

The difficulty of each hike in this book is rated by the following criteria:

Easy: Under 2 miles round-trip *and* under 500 feet elevation gain.

Moderate: 2 to 5 miles round-trip *or* 500 feet to 1,200 feet elevation gain.

More challenging: More than 5 miles but less than 8 miles round-trip *or* more than 1,200 feet but less than 2,000 feet elevation gain.

Very strenuous: More than 8 miles round-trip *or* 2,000 feet or more elevation gain.

Note that these ratings are a general guideline. In some cases, a hike might be rated higher or lower than these criteria based on the terrain. The elevation gain given for a hike is the total elevation that you climb, taking into account all ups and downs.

Hiking times are conservative. In general, super-fit expert hikers might be able to cover 2 miles per hour if the terrain is relatively smooth and not too steep and if they never stop moving. The average person usually hikes at half that speed, about 1 mile per hour. Some people swear by the formula half the total distance plus one hour for every 1,000 vertical feet. In other words, if a hike is 6 miles long and climbs 2,000 vertical feet, it will take five hours. In the end, hiking times are an educated guess and ultimately depend on how fit you are and how much you dally at each viewpoint.

Terrain can make a trail challenging. ▶

About the Maps

The overview map indicates major access roads to each trailhead and, possibly more important, the relative location of hikes to one another to help you plan a whole day or weekend of great hikes in one general vicinity.

For your own purposes, you may wish to copy the directions for the route onto a small sheet to help you while hiking, or photocopy the map and Miles and Directions to take with you. Otherwise, just slip the whole book in your pack and take it with you. Enjoy your time in the outdoors and remember to pack out what you pack in.

The route map is your guide to each hike. It shows the accessible roads and trails, water, landmarks, towns, and key navigational features. It also distinguishes trails from roads, and paved roads from unpaved roads. The selected route is highlighted.

The maps in this book are not intended to replace more-detailed agency maps, road maps, state atlases, and/or topographic maps, but they do indicate the general lay of the trail and its attractions to help you visualize and navigate its course.

Trail Finder

	Easy, Small Child Friendly	Dog Friendly	Cabins, Shelters	Tent sites	Trailhead Campground	Open Rock or Alpine Summit	Rock Perch, Dramatic Cliff, or Ridge Walk	Lake, Pond	Waterfall	Fire Tower or Viewing Platform
SOUTHERN GREEN MOUNTAINS: Massachusetts Border to Londonderry										
1. Bromley Mountain			•							•
2. Harmon Hill	•	•								
3. Haystack Mountain		•				•	•			
4. Lye Brook Falls	•	•							•	
5. Bourne Pond–Stratton Pond Loop		•	•	•				•		
6. Stratton Mountain–Stratton Pond Loop		•	•	•				•		•
SOUTH-CENTRAL GREEN MOUNTAINS: Danby to Killington										
7. Baker Peak–Griffith Lake Loop		•		•		•	•	•		
8. Deer Leap Outlook	•	•					•			
9. Killington Peak		•	•			•				closed
10. Little Rock Pond and Green Mountain		•	•	•		•	•	•		
11. Okemo Mountain		•								•
12. Pico Peak		•	•				•			•
13. White Rocks Cliffs		•	•				•		•	
14. White Rocks Ice Beds	•						•			

	Easy, Small Child Friendly	Dog Friendly	Cabins, Shelters	Tent sites	Trailhead Campground	Open Rock or Alpine Summit	Rock Perch, Dramatic Cliff, or Ridge Walk	Lake, Pond	Waterfall	Fire Tower or Viewing Platform
NORTH-CENTRAL GREEN MOUNTAINS: Brandon Gap to Huntington										
15. Mount Horrid's Great Cliffs	•	•					•			
16. Silver Lake		•		•	•			•		
17. Rattlesnake Cliffs and Mount Moosalamoo		•		•	•		•		•	
18. Abbey Pond	•	•						•		
19. Mount Abraham via the Long Trail		•	•			•				
20. Mount Abraham via the Battell Trail		•	•			•				
WATERBURY-STOWE AREA: Waterbury to Jeffersonville										
21. Elephant's Head Cliff–Sterling Pond Loop			•				•	•		
22. Camel's Hump via the Monroe Trail		•				•	•			
23. Camel's Hump via the Forest City Trail–Burrows Trail Loop		•	•			•	•			
24. Mount Elmore and Balanced Rock		•		•	•					•

	Easy, Small Child Friendly	Dog Friendly	Cabins, Shelters	Tent sites	Trailhead Campground	Open Rock or Alpine Summit	Rock Perch, Dramatic Cliff, or Ridge Walk	Lake, Pond	Waterfall	Fire Tower or Viewing Platform
25. Mount Hunger		●				●				
26. Stowe Pinnacle	●	●				●				
27. Mount Mansfield: The Forehead via Butler Lodge Trail–Maple Ridge Loop			●			●	●			
28. Mount Mansfield via the Sunset Ridge Trail		●			●	●	●			
29. Mount Mansfield via the Long Trail–South			●			●	●			
NORTHERN GREEN MOUNTAINS: Johnson to the Canadian Border										
30. Belvidere Mountain Loop		●	●				●	●		●
31. Jay Peak	●	●	●			●	●	●		
32. Mount Pisgah	●	●					●			
33. Wheeler Mountain Loop	●	●					●			
34. Bald Mountain (Westmore)	●	●	●							●
35. Devil's Gulch–Ritterbush Pond Loop			●				●	●		

Map Legend

Transportation

Interstate	15
U.S. Highway	27
State Road	19
Local/Forest Road	USFS 21
Dirt Road	=====
Railroad	⊢—┼—┼—┤
Featured Trail	▬ ▬ ▬ ▬
Other Trail	– – – – – –

Hydrology

Lake/Pond	
River/Brook	
Waterfall	

Land Use

State Park	

True North
(Magnetic North is
approximately 15.5° East)

N

Symbols

Campground	▲
Campsite (back country)	▲ ▲
Point of Interest	■
Mountain/Peak	▲
Parking	P
Picnic Area	⊞
Tower	🗼
City/Town	○
Trailhead (start)	❺
Bridge	)(
Pass/Gap	)(
Ranger Station	
Bench	
Boat Launch	
Viewpoint	
Scale	0 Kilometer 1 0 Mile 1

Southern Green Mountains

Massachusetts Border to Londonderry

1 Bromley Mountain via the Appalachian Trail/Long Trail

A gradual yet steady climb through a hardwood forest to a viewing platform at the top of the Bromley Ski Area. Passes one of the newer lodges on the Appalachian Trail (AT)/Long Trail (LT) in Vermont. Excellent view, particularly toward Stratton to the south.

General location: Peru
Distance: 5.6 miles out and back
Approximate hiking time: 4.5 hours
Difficulty: More challenging
Highest elevation: 3,260 feet
Elevation gain: 1,460 feet

Canine compatibility: Dog friendly
Trail contact: Green Mountain Club, (802) 244-7037, www.greenmountainclub.org; Green Mountain National Forest, Manchester District, (802) 362-2307, www.fs.fed.us/gmfl
Maps: USGS Peru Quad

Finding the trailhead: From Manchester, take Route 30/11 east toward the Bromley Ski Area. Look for the large trailhead parking lot on the left (north) side of Route 11 where the AT/LT crosses the road.

The Hike

There are two out-and-back approaches to Bromley, both on the AT/LT (white blazes). The approach from the south is 0.3 mile longer, but it has some interesting points along the way; namely, Bromley Brook, a nice place to pause if you are hiking with a dog, and Bromley Shelter, where you can spend the night.

Hiking up Bromley Mountain feels easier than the distance might suggest. It is a good option if you are not quite up to either of the two nearby giants, Mount Equinox and Stratton Mountain, but still want a hike to an expansive view. Most of the route is in the Green Mountain National Forest, but the summit lies in Hapgood State Forest, which is under long-term lease to the Bromley Ski Area.

From the trailhead, take the AT/LT–North, which begins as a dirt road at the east end of the elongated parking lot. After only 50 yards, turn left onto a footpath, crossing a stream via a curious steel girder placed there as a bridge.

The approach to the mountain is long and flat through an airy hardwood forest. At 0.5 mile, the trail crosses Bromley Brook. There can be muddy sections over the next mile or so, but most of it is easily avoided thanks to bog bridges (puncheon) or by rock hopping.

At 1.4 miles, the trail begins to climb gently to a three-way intersection, which is really just the spur to Bromley Shelter and its outhouse. Go left (north) to reach the summit. Backpackers planning to sleep at Bromley Shelter should bear right (southeast) to drop their packs at the shelter before heading to the top. Bromley Shelter was rebuilt in 2003 and is a lean-to with a picnic table, composting privy, and sleeping "shelves" that span the width of the shelter.

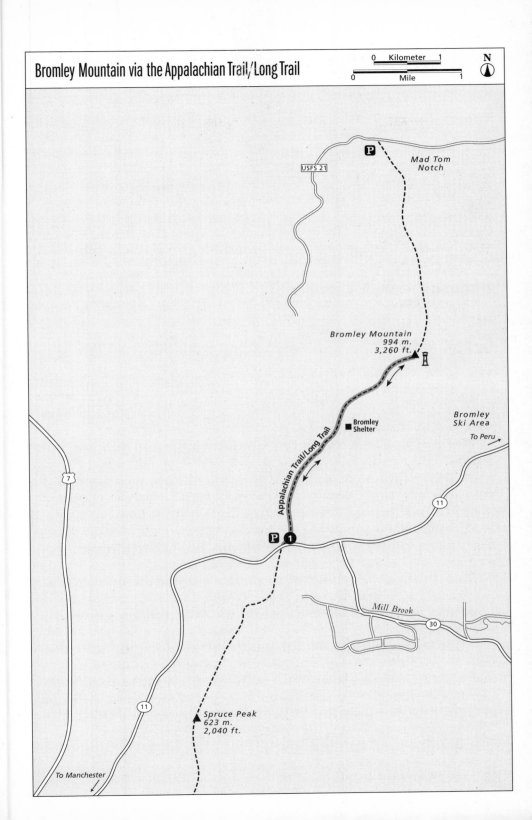

Bromley Mountain via the Appalachian Trail/Long Trail

0 Kilometer 1

0 Mile 1

N

Mad Tom Notch

USFS 21

Bromley Mountain
994 m.
3,260 ft.

Bromley Shelter

Bromley Ski Area

To Peru

Appalachian Trail/Long Trail

7

11

11

30

Mill Brook

Spruce Peak
623 m.
2,040 ft.

To Manchester

A "GREEN" START

Hapgood State Forest was named after Marshel J. Hapgood, who is credited with the idea of establishing a federal forest reserve in Vermont, which ultimately became Green Mountain National Forest. Hapgood owned several mills that made wood products. He was an early proponent of selective logging to ensure regeneration of trees and to limit erosion at a time when clear-cutting without planned revegetation was the norm. In 1905 he offered to sell his land near Bromley Mountain, at a below-market price, to the Teddy Roosevelt administration. It took another twenty-seven years for the purchase to happen. This was the first tract of land that the U.S. government acquired in Vermont for the purpose of conservation. Hapgood's initiative for the public to own and conserve Vermont's mountains and upland forests continues to benefit hikers today.

Follow the AT/LT another 0.3 mile to a vista, then up through a fern forest. At 2.5 miles, the trail breaks out onto the Run Around ski trail. Turn left, heading upward on the footpath through the center of the grassy ski trail.

The top of the mountain is an open meadow with more ski trails heading off in several directions. Rather than a fire tower, there is a broad viewing platform with chicken wire below the railings and risers on the backs of the stairs. Stratton Mountain dominates the view across the valley, but look around: The 360-degree view is one of the best in southern Vermont.

Return by the same route.

Miles and Directions

0.0 Start at the trailhead for the AT/LT-North at the east end of the trailhead parking lot.

0.5 Cross Bromley Brook.

1.4 Turn left (north) at the three-way intersection near Bromley Shelter.

1.7 First scenic vista.

2.5 Turn left (north) onto the Run Around ski trail.

2.8 SUMMIT! Return by the same route.

5.6 Arrive back at the trailhead.

◀ *AT/LT to Bromley Mountain.*

2 Harmon Hill via the Appalachian Trail/Long Trail

Popular trek through an airy hardwood forest to a landmark on the Appalachian Trail, with views of the nearby Bennington area and Taconic Range to the west. Wildflowers in May include trout lily (dog-toothed violet), squirrel corn, spring beauties, purple trillium, hobblebush, yellow violets, bellwort.

General location: Bennington
Distance: 3.4 miles out and back
Approximate hiking time: 3 hours
Difficulty: Moderate
Highest elevation: 2,325 feet
Elevation gain: 1,265 feet
Canine compatibility: Dog friendly. Dogs should be under control at all times and on leash around other hikers. No reliable water, though the riverlike City Stream flows past the parking lot, offering a refreshing spot for your dog to cool off after the hike.

Trail contact: Green Mountain Club, (802) 244-7037, www.greenmountainclub.org; Green Mountain National Forest, Manchester District, (802) 362-2307, www.fs.fed.us/gmfl

Maps: USGS Woodford, Bennington, Pownal Quads

Finding the trailhead: From the junction of U.S. Highway 7 and Route 9 in Bennington, travel east on Route 9 toward Wilmington for 4.9 miles. Trailhead parking is on the north (left) side of the road. Carefully cross the road to the trailhead for the Appalachian Trail (AT)/Long Trail (LT)–South. From the junction of Routes 9 and 100 in Wilmington, travel west on Route 9 for 15.5 miles. Trailhead parking is on the right side of the road.

The Hike

Harmon Hill was likely named for the prominent Harmon family of the town of Rupert in Bennington County. Reuben Harmon Jr., a member of the Vermont General Assembly, was authorized to mine and mint copper coins in this region as part of Vermont's proclamation as an independent republic prior to its becoming the fourteenth state in 1791.

The climb up Harmon Hill starts out with a cardio bang, but ends with a casual lilt. While the views from the summit are not particularly dramatic, it is a pleasing destination at the end of a nice woodland walk.

Enter the woods on the AT/LT–South (white blazes). The path climbs steeply up a long series of stone steps and well-placed rocks, in a show of expert trail work, and gains elevation quickly. By 0.2 mile, it levels off and bends right (west), continuing upward but in a series of waves and at a more moderate incline.

At about 0.4 mile, the trail bends back to the left (south). It then heads upward through the hardwood forest via several elongated switchbacks with rock steps in steeper sections.

By 0.8 mile, the trail crests a plateau, then meanders in a westerly direction, slightly downhill, and crosses a narrow streamlet. The footing is noticeably smoother. In May

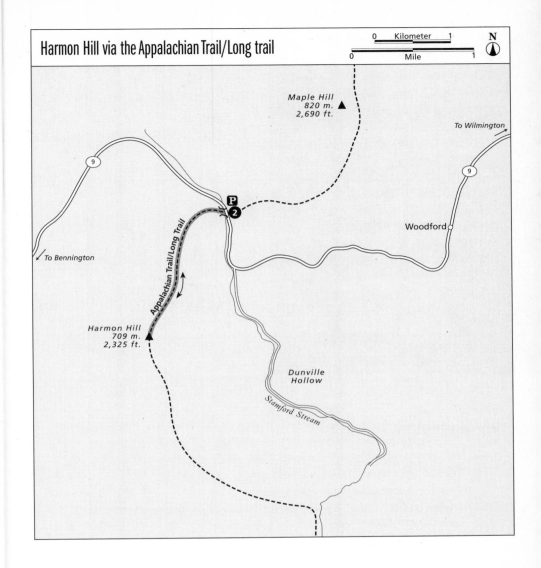

Harmon Hill via the Appalachian Trail/Long trail

Maple Hill
820 m.
2,690 ft.

To Wilmington

9

9

To Bennington

Appalachian Trail/Long Trail

Woodford

Harmon Hill
709 m.
2,325 ft.

Dunville
Hollow

Stamford Stream

the woods here are carpeted with yellow trout lilies (also called dog-toothed violets), with their mottled green and brown leaves.

At about 1.2 miles, the trail bends left (south) again, crossing a series of puncheon over a muddy area. From here it climbs gently for the remainder of the route. Spring beauties take over as the dominant ground cover under the trees. Their small white and pink flowers cause the forest floor to shimmer when they bloom during the spring.

Harmon Hill puncheon.

The trail reaches the summit of Harmon Hill at 1.7 miles. A green box marks the end of the Pioneer Valley section of the Long Trail and the start of the Bennington section. It also notes the three-quarter point of the Appalachian Trail, 1,563 miles from Springer Mountain, Georgia, and 557 miles to Mount Katadin, Maine. Char marks on some of the trees are evidence of the periodic burns by the Forest Service to help maintain the grassy summit.

From the sign, grassy paths fan out in each direction, revealing views of nearby hills. The view to the west is the best of nearby Mount Anthony and the Taconic Range beyond, the Bennington area, and the towering monument commemorating the Revolutionary War Battle of Bennington in 1777.

Return by the same route.

Miles and Directions

0.0 Start at the trailhead for the AT/LT–South. Climb steeply up a rocky slope.

0.2 Level off briefly, bending to the west. Continue to climb in waves.

0.4 Bend back south, ascending elongated switchbacks.

0.8 Reach a plateau. Footing becomes smoother through an airy hardwood forest in a predominantly westward direction.

1.2 Bend south again, crossing a series of puncheon.

1.7 SUMMIT! Marked by a sign and a green box. Return by the same route.

3.4 Arrive back at the trailhead.

3 Haystack Mountain via the Haystack Mountain Trail

A pleasant, gradual climb to a small rocky summit with excellent views, especially to the east into New Hampshire. The rocky perch at the summit over Haystack Pond is a perfect picnic spot.

General location: Wilmington
Distance: 4.8 miles out and back
Approximate hiking time: 3 hours
Difficulty: Moderate
Highest elevation: 3,420 feet
Elevation gain: 1,020 feet

Canine compatibility: Dog friendly. Excellent route for puppies and senior dogs. Carry water.
Trail contact: Green Mountain National Forest, Manchester District, (802) 362-2307, www.fs.fed.us/r9/gmfl
Maps: USGS Mount Snow Quad

Finding the trailhead: From Route 9 west of Wilmington, turn right onto Chimney Hill Road. Turn right on Binney Brook Road and follow it uphill through a residential development. Turn left on Upper Dam Road. The trailhead and parking are on the right, after the turn onto Upper Dam Road.

The Hike

Haystack Mountain is a common name for peaks in the Northeast. The name comes from the mountain's shape, which resembles a giant stack of hay. During the 1800s much of Vermont's woodlands were cleared for farming. While most of those fields have grown back into forest, and the remaining farmers now make large bales instead

View of Haystack Pond from the summit of Haystack Mountain.

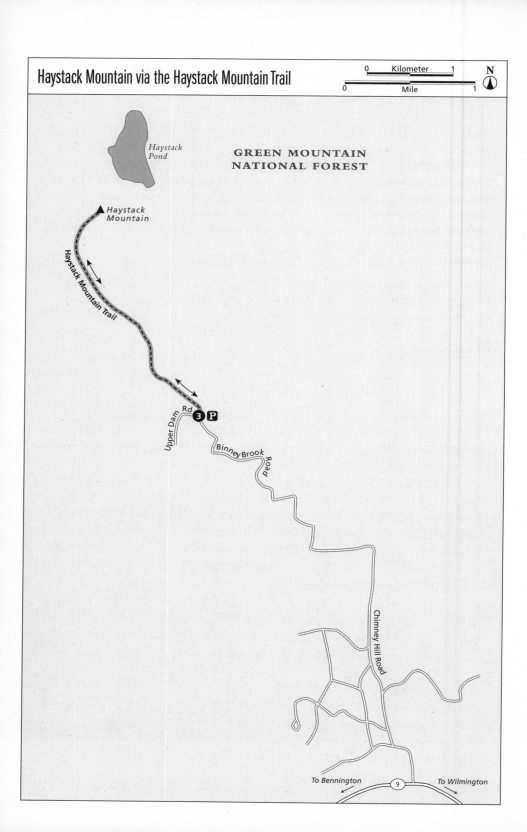

Haystack Mountain via the Haystack Mountain Trail

0 Kilometer 1
0 Mile 1

N

Haystack Pond

GREEN MOUNTAIN NATIONAL FOREST

▲ *Haystack Mountain*

Haystack Mountain Trail

Upper Dam Rd

3 P

Binney Brook Road

Chimney Hill Road

To Bennington 9 To Wilmington

of stacks of hay, the mountains of that shape remain as a reminder of this heritage.

There are three Haystack Mountains with hiking trails in Vermont. Two are in the Northeast Kingdom, one near Jay Peak and one near Lake Willoughby. The third, described here, is at the opposite end of the state near Mount Snow.

This Haystack Mountain is well-known among the region's skiers as a struggling satellite ski area to giant Mount Snow. From a hiker's point of view, whatever Haystack lacks as a ski area, it more than makes up for as a hiking destination. While Mount Snow is bigger, its trail system is popular for mountain biking. The Haystack Mountain Trail (blue blazes) is mainly used as a footpath and thus much more conducive to an invigorating yet peaceful walk in the woods.

The trail begins on a gravel road. Walk around the gate partway up the initial incline, continuing along the road.

At 0.4 mile, the trail turns left over a streamlet onto a wide footpath, leaving the woods road behind. After descending through a muddy area, the path ascends gently through hardwoods and then flattens out heading north.

At 1.0 mile, the trail resumes its gentle ascent, bending to the right. *Note:* The trail markers in this section are shaped like blue diamonds rather than the vertical rectangles more common to Vermont's trails.

At 1.6 miles, the trail comes to another plateau. The canopy opens up over the trail as it passes through a hedge of wild blackberry bushes. A little while later, it crosses another muddy area, then ascends gently again. The trail becomes rockier, with water trickling down it unless the weather has been unusually dry.

At 2.0 miles, a small rock cairn blocks the middle of the trail, and a yellow arrow signals a 90-degree turn to the right up a short, steep incline. The trail soon moderates again, winding up the hill.

At 2.4 miles, the trail comes to a large rock as hardwoods turn to firs. Scramble over it to the top! Haystack Pond lies about 500 feet below the summit, with Mount Monadnock in New Hampshire directly ahead to the east. The Mount Snow ski area is obvious to the left (north). On a clear day, Killington and the Coolidge Range are also visible to the north beyond Mount Snow. Wachusett Mountain and Greylock in Massachusetts lie on the southern horizon.

Return by the same route.

Miles and Directions

0.0 Start at the Haystack Mountain trailhead. Walk around the gate on a gravel road.

0.4 Turn left off the gravel road onto a wide footpath, which becomes flat after an initial moderate ascent.

1.0 Resume a gentle ascent.

1.6 Traverse a plateau. Break in the forest canopy.

2.0 Turn right at the rock cairn up a short, steep incline.

2.4 SUMMIT! Return by the same route.

4.8 Arrive back at the trailhead.

4 Lye Brook Falls via the Lye Brook Trail

A serene woodland walk to a spectacular 160-foot waterfall, one of the tallest in Vermont.

General location: Manchester
Distance: 4.6 miles out and back
Approximate hiking time: 3.5 hours
Difficulty: Moderate
Highest elevation: 1,350 feet
Elevation gain: 1,000 feet
Canine compatibility: Dog friendly. Keep dogs

on a short leash near the cliffs around the waterfall.
Trail contact: Green Mountain Club, (802) 244-7037, www.greenmountainclub.org; Green Mountain National Forest, Manchester Office, (802) 362-2307, www.fs.fed.us/gmfl
Maps: USGS Manchester (VT) Quad

Finding the trailhead: From U.S. Highway 7 in Manchester, take Route 30/11 east for 0.4 mile. Take a hard right (southwest) on East Manchester Road. Go 1.2 miles and turn left (south) on Glen Road. Glen Road immediately crosses a bridge, turns to dirt, and comes to a fork. Bear right at the fork nearest the sign LYE BROOK WILDERNESS ENTRY 7. Continue 0.4 mile to a dead-end circle. The trailhead is on the southeastern side of the circle.

The Hike

The route to Lye Brook Falls along the Lye Brook Trail (blue blazes) is a wonderful half-day introduction to hiking. The trail is broad and follows an old logging road and a railroad bed. It climbs gently, gaining about 800 feet from the trailhead to the spur to the falls, passing through peaceful forest. It then drops 200 feet on a moderate incline to the falls. Save this hike for after a rainstorm, as the falls dry to a less impressive trickle by mid-June.

From the trailhead, the path starts out over giant cobblestone-like rocks, but after a few moments, it bends to the right (south) and becomes a smooth woods road, where it is easy to move quickly if you are pushed for time.

At about 0.4 mile, the trail passes a washout where you can see Lye Brook at the bottom of the steep, eroded bank. The sign-in box for the Lye Brook Wilderness Area is around the bend, at 0.5 mile. Sign in, then continue around another bend to find an unusually long, straight corridor. The rest of the route follows this former railroad bed, which was used for logging. Years ago the tracks passed the base of Lye Brook Falls on a trestle, hence the original name of the waterfall, Trestle Falls.

At 0.6 mile, the trail crosses the first of two streamlets, then begins to climb more noticeably uphill. The tree branches close in more along this section of the trail.

At 1.3 miles, the trail bends left (northeast) over a substantial rock water bar, then winds back to its original direction. At the top of the rise is another double stream crossing, between which the path seems like a rocky streambed itself.

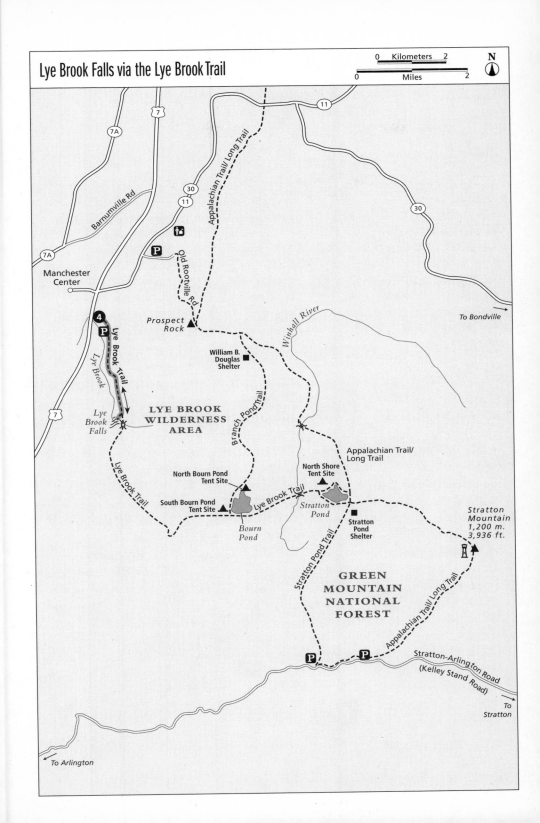

Lye Brook Falls via the Lye Brook Trail

Kilometers
Miles

N

To Bondville

7

7A

7A

Manchester Center

30

11

Barnumville Rd

11

30

Appalachian Trail/Long Trail

Old Rootville Rd

Prospect Rock

Winhall River

William B. Douglas Shelter

4

P

Lye Brook Trail

Lye Brook

Lye Brook Falls

LYE BROOK WILDERNESS AREA

Branch Pond Trail

Appalachian Trail/Long Trail

North Bourn Pond Tent Site

North Shore Tent Site

South Bourn Pond Tent Site

Lye Brook Trail

Stratton Pond

Stratton Pond Shelter

Stratton Mountain 1,200 m. 3,936 ft.

Bourn Pond

Lye Brook Trail

Stratton Pond Trail

GREEN MOUNTAIN NATIONAL FOREST

Appalachian Trail/Long Trail

P

P

Stratton-Arlington Road (Kelley Stand Road)

To Stratton

To Arlington

After the second streamlet, the trail levels off, passing through a stand of hemlocks as it traverses the side of Lye Brook Hollow, a shallow ravine. The hillside above looks like an overgrown scree field, though the path underfoot is smooth.

At 1.8 miles, the trail crosses a slightly wider stream on large mossy rocks and then comes to the junction with the spur to Lye Brook Falls. Bear right (southwest) at the fork. The trail feels slightly narrower as it heads downhill, dropping down the side of the ravine, but it is a continuation of the same railroad bed. After rain, sections of the trail can be rather wet, where water flows off the rock outcroppings beside the path.

At 2.3 miles, the official spur trail ends at a rocky perch over the base of Lye Brook Falls. You can climb partway up the left side of the cascade via a narrow path that passes another rocky perch, an excellent place to view the tumbling white water apart from other visitors on the larger rock below. Most of the year, the falls are not a raging torrent. The water flows down the rocks like a broad layer of white satin coating a hundred steps, which is what makes this such a beautiful, relaxing place to visit.

Return by the same route.

Miles and Directions

0.0 Start at the trailhead for the Lye Brook Trail. Begin climbing over large cobble-like rocks.

0.4 Pass a washout with a view of Lye Brook below.

0.5 Sign in at the boundary of the Lye Brook Wilderness Area.

0.6 Cross two streamlets, then climb more noticeably uphill.

1.3 Turn left (northeast) over a substantial rock water bar, then cross two more streamlets at the top of the rise.

1.8 Cross a wider stream on mossy rocks. Bear right at the fork onto the spur trail to Lye Brook Falls, heading downhill.

2.3 WATERFALL! Return by the same route.

4.6 Arrive back at the trailhead.

◀ *Hikers beside Lye Brook Falls.*

5 Bourn Pond-Stratton Pond Loop

Overnight backpacking through a microburst area and past two ponds, followed by a long peaceful forest walk through Lye Brook Wilderness.

General location: Manchester
Distance: 16.5-mile lollipop
Approximate hiking time: 2–3 days
Difficulty: Moderate
Highest elevation: 2,250 feet
Elevation gain: 1,165 feet
Canine compatibility: Dog friendly

Trail contact: Green Mountain Club, (802) 244-7037, www.greenmountainclub.org; Green Mountain National Forest, Manchester District, (802) 362-2307, www.fs.fed.us/gmfl
Maps: USGS Stratton Mountain, Sunderland, Peru, and Manchester Quads

Finding the trailhead: From the Green Mountain National Forest ranger office on Route 30/11 in Manchester Depot, head downhill (southwest) 0.6 mile toward Manchester. Turn south on East Manchester Road, then immediately bear left (southeast) on Old Rootville Road (dirt). Go 0.5 mile to the end of the drivable portion of the road. The small turnout on the right is the trailhead parking area.

The Hike

The hike to Bourn Pond and Stratton Pond is an excellent way to traverse through the heart of the Lye Brook Wilderness. There are lengthy stretches through pristine woodlands on this trek, but the big rewards are an early view from Prospect Rock above Manchester and then your choice of shelters or pond-side tent sites. This loop hike is described here as a two-day outing, but many extend it to three days (or longer), base camping at either Bourn Pond or Stratton Pond, then using the extra day to either climb Stratton Mountain or just enjoy some swimming and fishing.

Day One

From the parking area, head up the gravel continuation of Old Rootville Road (aka Prospect Rock Trail), passing the sign for the Green Mountain National Forest. The road ascends an unrelenting 1,000 feet, paralleling Bourn Brook on your right.

At about 1.5 miles, the road levels off. You can glimpse Mount Equinox and the Taconic Range to your right (west) through the trees.

At 1.8 miles, the Prospect Rock Trail ends at the Appalachian Trail/Long Trail (AT/LT; white blazes). The AT/LT–North departs the road to the left, and the road becomes the AT/LT–South. It's easy to miss the short spur to Prospect Rock (blue blazes), which is on the right, as the sign announcing this rocky perch is about 15 feet high on a white birch tree. The sign at eye level merely says LOOK UP. Prospect Rock is a popular destination in its own right for those short on time but who want a nice view. The hulking Mount Equinox is directly across the Otter Creek Valley, a large section of which lies before you to the north.

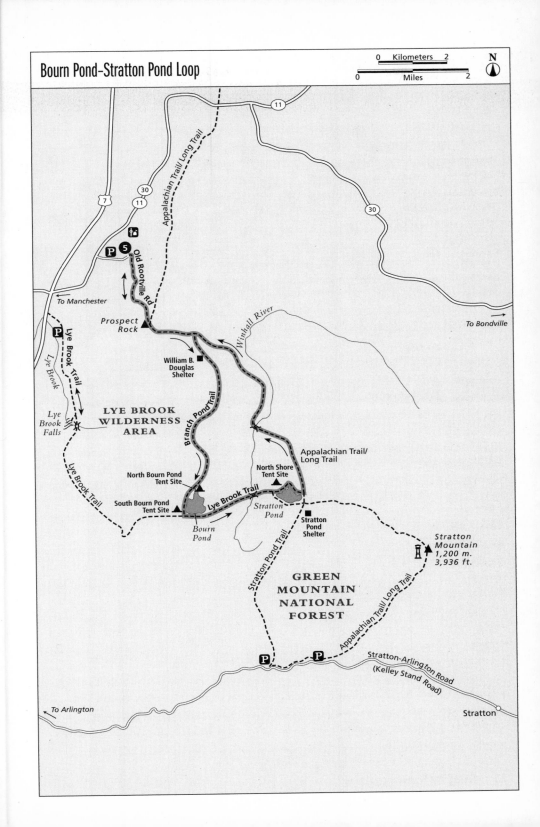

Bourn Pond-Stratton Pond Loop

0 Kilometers 2

0 Miles 2

N

To Manchester

Old Rootville Rd

Prospect Rock

Appalachian Trail/ Long Trail

Winhall River

William B. Douglas Shelter

Lye Brook Trail

Lye Brook

Lye Brook Falls

LYE BROOK WILDERNESS AREA

Branch Pond Trail

Lye Brook Trail

North Bourn Pond Tent Site

North Shore Tent Site

Appalachian Trail/ Long Trail

South Bourn Pond Tent Site

Lye Brook Trail

Bourn Pond

Stratton Pond

Stratton Pond Shelter

Stratton Mountain 1,200 m. 3,936 ft.

Stratton Pond Trail

GREEN MOUNTAIN NATIONAL FOREST

Appalachian Trail/ Long Trail

To Bondville

To Arlington

Stratton-Arlington Road (Kelley Stand Road)

Stratton

The author on the bridge across the Windhall River, in the Lye Brook Wilderness.

From Prospect Rock, continue up the road, soon coming to a gate. Walk around the gate and follow the road until it takes a sharp bend to the left up a steep incline. Ignore the turn and head straight into the woods onto a footpath. After about 50 yards, the trail passes a NATIONAL FOREST WILDERNESS sign and arrives at an unofficial junction. Continue straight ahead on the AT/LT–South, ignoring the overgrown trail on the left.

At 2.7 miles, the trail crosses a tributary of Bourn Brook on a footbridge and ascends a small rise to the junction with the Branch Pond Trail. You will close the loop at this intersection tomorrow.

Bear right (south) on Branch Pond Trail, which officially enters the Lye Brook Wilderness. The route crosses puncheon as it traverses through the hardwood forest, with a jewelweed carpet on either side of the boards. After a long, gradual descent, the trail crosses more puncheon and then arrives at Douglas Shelter at 3.2 miles.

The shelter is a typical three-sided lean-to in a small clearing. It was built in 1956 and renovated in 2005. If you are planning a couple nights in the Lye Brook Wilderness and get a late start, this is a good place to sleep the first night.

The trail crosses the front of the shelter and then heads southeast back into the woods.

From here it is a pleasant, rolling 3-mile walk through the woods to Bourn Pond. The trail passes through a small clearing filled with head-high goldenrod. It is lesser used than the AT/LT and is prime moose habitat. Constant signs of these large ungulates can be found here, including hand-size hoofprints and scat. At one point the trail dips down to a stream, then continues along its left bank. Farther along there are a couple of unaided stream crossings, as bridges are generally not constructed in designated wilderness areas.

At 6.2 miles, the trail reaches the northern end of Bourn Pond, which is visible across the marsh grass through the trees. The trail generally follows the western shoreline of the pond, though it swings away from the water briefly on old log ties until it meets the spur to the North Bourn Pond tent site. Continue straight on the Branch Pond Trail–South. Moments later, the trail comes alongside the water, soon passing a couple of beautiful pond-side primitive campsites.

At 6.7 miles, the Branch Pond Trail meets the Lye Brook Trail, which enters from the right (west). The site of the former South Bourn Pond shelter, now a primitive campsite, is also just to the right. The two trails run concurrently to the left (east) for about 50 yards, then the Branch Pond Trail splits off to the right, continuing south. Stay on the Lye Brook Trail, heading east.

At 7.7 miles, the trail suddenly breaks out of the forest canopy and enters a large area of fallen trees. In 2006 a microburst hit the area, creating the expansive blowdown. The trail makes its way through the blowdown, where wild raspberry bushes abound among the jumble of tree trunks. At the opposite side of the microburst, the trail crosses a small backwater, then passes out of the Lye Brook Wilderness.

The trail reenters the forest and then turns sharply left (west) over a small footbridge. It climbs a low hillside and reaches the western corner of Stratton Pond and the junction with the North Shore Trail at 8.5 miles. Turn left (east) on the North Shore Trail. The trail passes the water source for the tent site and a small grassy opening on the shore of the pond, which is the best access into the water for a

Bourn Pond.

swim. The top of Stratton Mountain's gondola and the fire tower sit like two crowns on the elongated peak on the opposite shoreline. Listen for the call of the loons and watch for a brook trout rising on the water.

The North Shore tent site is just ahead on the left, partway along a stretch of puncheon. The site has several tent platforms available on a first-come, first-served basis. Expect a caretaker from the Green Mountain Club to visit during the summer and early fall to exchange pleasantries about your hike and to collect the site fee; the charge is per person. There's also a fire pit for a campfire.

Day Two

From the North Shore tent site, continue along the shoreline trail, reaching the junction with the AT/LT at 9.2 miles on the northeastern side of the pond. Turn left (north) on the AT/LT, climbing gently away from the pond and passing the Catamount Trail on your right. A few moments later, the trail reenters the Lye Brook Wilderness. From here it rolls at length through the airy forest.

At about 11.0 miles, the forest monotony is broken by a well-constructed footbridge over the Winhall River. At 12.2 miles, the trail takes a noticeable turn to the left (west) at a low, viewless pinnacle in the woods.

The loop finally closes at the junction with the Branch Pond Trail at 13.8 miles. From here retrace back to the Old Rootville Road/Prospect Rock Trail, passing Prospect Rock and descending back to the trailhead at 16.5 miles.

Miles and Directions

0.0 Start at the trailhead for the Prospect Rock Trail on Old Rootville Road.

1.8 The AT/LT-North departs to the left; a short spur to Prospect Rock is on the right. Continue up the road, now the AT/LT-South.

2.7 Bear right (south) at the junction of the AT/LT and Branch Pond Trail onto the Branch Pond Trail.

3.2 Pass Douglas Shelter.

6.2 Reach North Bourn Pond tent site.

6.7 Junction with Lye Brook Trail. South Bourn Pond tent site is on the right. Turn left onto the Lye Brook Trail, heading east.

7.7 Pass through an expansive blowdown.

8.5 Turn left (east) onto the North Shore Trail at the western shoreline of Stratton Pond and the North Shore tent site.

9.2 Continue along the northern shoreline of Stratton Pond to the junction with the AT/LT. Turn left (north) onto the AT/LT, reentering the Lye Brook Wilderness.

13.8 Close the loop at junction with Branch Pond Trail.

14.7 Pass by Prospect Rock again. The AT/LT-North departs road on right. Follow the Old Rootsville Road back to the trailhead.

16.5 Arrive back at the trailhead.

6 Stratton Mountain–Stratton Pond Loop

A long day hike or overnight backpacking trip over the tallest peak in southern Vermont and by the largest body of water on the Long Trail. Historic fire tower on summit of Stratton with sweeping 360-degree view.

General location: Stratton
Distance: 11.5-mile loop
Approximate hiking time: 8 hours (day hike); 2 days (backpacking)
Difficulty: Very strenuous day hike (due to length); moderate backpacking trip
Highest elevation: 3,936 feet

Elevation gain: 1,910 feet
Canine compatibility: Dog friendly
Trail contact: Green Mountain Club, (802) 244-7037, www.greenmountainclub.org; Green Mountain National Forest, Manchester District, (802) 362-2307, www.fs.fed.us/r9/gmfl
Map: USGS Stratton Mountain Quad

Finding the trailhead: From the village of Stratton—not the ski resort—drive 3.0 miles west toward Arlington on Stratton-Arlington Road/Kelley Stand Road (closed in winter). The trailhead for the Appalachian Trail/Long Trail (AT/LT) is on the north side of the road just past the trailhead for Grout Pond.

The Hike

The Stratton Mountain–Stratton Pond Loop is one of Vermont's classic hiking routes. While it is lengthy mileage-wise as a day hike, the footing is generally good and the elevation gain reasonable for the distance. However, if you have the time, it's worth planning a night by Stratton Pond either in the shelter or at one of the tent sites. The 46-acre pond is like a small lake and an endless source of backcountry entertainment. You can explore the entire circumference, take a dip, go fishing for brook trout or bullhead, or simply relax by your tent as you listen to the waves gently lap the shoreline.

The elevation gain on the loop is up Stratton Mountain, which is of historical significance to hikers on the East Coast. It was atop Stratton Mountain in 1921 that Benton McKaye first conceived of the Appalachian Trail, from Georgia to Maine. His inspiration came from another hiker, James Taylor, who in 1909 first proposed a "long trail" to link the main peaks of the Green Mountains along the entire length of Vermont. A significant portion of the Stratton Mountain–Stratton Pond Loop is on the AT/LT (white blazes).

From the trailhead on Kelley Stand Road, follow the AT/LT–North into the woods. The trail comes immediately to a fork. Bear right, traversing a muddy area.

At 0.4 mile, the trail crosses a streamlet and starts to climb easily along a woods road. It crosses several stretches of puncheon as it traverses slightly downhill, heading toward the mountain. Watch the white blazes carefully, as many old logging roads crisscross the trail here.

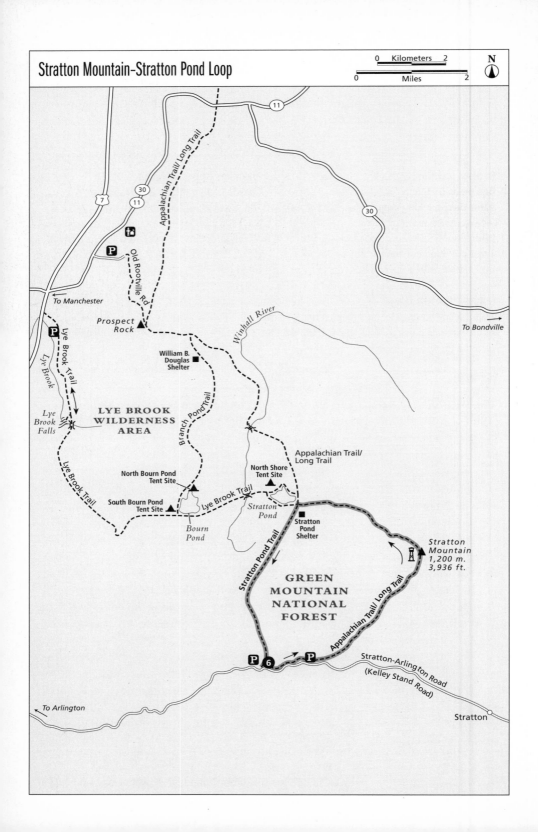

Stratton Mountain-Stratton Pond Loop

0 Kilometers 2
0 Miles 2

N

11

30

7
11

Appalachian Trail/ Long Trail

Old Rootville Rd

→ To Manchester

Prospect Rock

Winhall River

→ To Bondville

P

Lye Brook Trail

Lye Brook

Lye Brook Falls

William B. Douglas Shelter

LYE BROOK WILDERNESS AREA

Branch Pond Trail

Lye Brook Trail

Appalachian Trail/ Long Trail

North Bourn Pond Tent Site

North Shore Tent Site

South Bourn Pond Tent Site

Lye Brook Trail

Bourn Pond

Stratton Pond

Stratton Pond Shelter

Stratton Pond Trail

Stratton Mountain 1,200 m. 3,936 ft.

GREEN MOUNTAIN NATIONAL FOREST

Appalachian Trail/ Long Trail

P 6 P

Stratton-Arlington Road (Kelley Stand Road)

→ To Arlington

Stratton

Stratton Pond Shelter.

At 1.2 miles, the trail bends to the right (east) and climbs gently again over a knoll. It crosses several streamlets as it dips and bends, alternating between mellow climbing and flat walking.

At 1.9 miles, the climb becomes more persistent and rocky before flattening out again. It travels along a hillside, generally heading northward.

By 2.9 miles, the trail reaches an upland plateau. The trees become noticeably lower and thinner, and softwoods take over.

The miles go by quickly on this low-angle ascent. Nothing about the trail is steep or tricky. By 3.6 miles, the trail gets rockier again.

At 3.8 miles, the trail passes a white cabin on the summit of Stratton Mountain, which is reserved for a caretaker from the Green Mountain Club. The fire tower is directly ahead at the other end of the grassy clearing. Built in 1914, the original cabin atop the tower was replaced in 1934 with the current one. The Stratton fire tower is a designated National Historic Landmark. From its small metal cabin 55 feet above the ground, you can see the top of the ski area's gondola, 0.8 mile away on Stratton's north peak. The view from the tower extends into five states. Mount Snow is clearly visible to the south. Mount Monadnock in New Hampshire lies to the southeast, with Mount Ascutney to the northeast and Mount Equinox to the west. Stratton Pond is nearby to the northwest.

From the base of the fire tower, turn left and begin the descent toward Stratton Pond. At 4.1 miles, the trail bends to the left down wooden steps as it winds off the peak and reenters the hardwoods.

At 5.8 miles, the trail bends to the west, then crosses a logging road. It traverses a long, muddy area, eventually crossing a stream on a bridge. From the bridge, it climbs gently to a fork with an older trail. Bear right at the fork, heading uphill.

At 6.8 miles, the trail comes to the junction with the Stratton Pond Trail. Turn right toward Stratton Pond, continuing on the AT/LT–North a short way to the water's edge. Stratton Pond receives the heaviest use of any body of water on the Long Trail, particularly during the summer. However, if you trek there midweek after Labor Day, you'll likely be alone. Camping is only allowed at the shelter and designated tent sites. There is a small nightly fee per person, which helps defray the costs of managing the AT/LT in Vermont. The Green Mountain Club stations a caretaker at the pond during the summer, not only to collect camping fees, but also to maintain trails, compost sewage, and educate people about the area and how to be a low-impact hiker.

From Stratton Pond, backtrack the short distance to the junction of the AT/LT and the Stratton Pond Trail, continuing straight ahead on the Stratton Pond Trail (blue blazes). At the top of the next rise, the trail turns right, bending right past the short spur to Stratton Pond Shelter (straight ahead). Built in 1999, the shelter is an oversize lean-to, open on one side, with bunk platforms and a sleeping loft above a picnic table.

At 7.9 miles, the trail crosses the first of many puncheon as it heads gently downward.

At 9.0 miles, the trail crosses a woods road, then continues its long traverse over more puncheon, finally reaching Kelley Stand Road at 10.6 miles, though not your car. Turn left (east) and walk along the dirt road for another 0.9 mile, closing the loop where you started at the AT/LT trailhead.

Miles and Directions

0.0   Start at the trailhead for the AT/LT-North. Bear right at the fork, traversing a muddy area.

0.4   Cross a streamlet and then begin a gentle climb on a woods road.

1.2   Bend east, climbing over a knoll.

1.9   More persistent climb, then level again heading northward.

2.9   Reach a plateau. Trees get smaller with more softwoods.

3.6   Trail becomes noticeably rockier.

3.8   SUMMIT! Pass by the caretaker's cabin to the fire tower. Turn left (northwest) at the fire tower and begin the descent to Stratton Pond.

5.8   Bend west, crossing a logging road.

6.8   POND! Turn right at the junction with the Stratton Pond Trail, staying on the AT/LT-North a short way to the shoreline of Stratton Pond. Retrace the short distance back to the junction with the Stratton Pond Trail. Head south on the Stratton Pond Trail.

7.9   Cross the first of many puncheon.

9.0   Cross a woods road and then more puncheon.

10.6 Turn left (east) onto Kelley Stand Road.

11.5 Close the loop at your starting point, the trailhead for the AT/LT-North.

Pico Peak ▶

South-Central
Green Mountains

Danby to Killington

7 Baker Peak-Griffith Lake Loop

The perfect combo hike to both a scenic pond with waterfront tent sites and an open rock summit in the heart of the Big Branch Wilderness. Views north and south along the Otter Creek Valley.

General location: Danby
Distance: 8.6-mile lollipop
Approximate hiking time: 6.5 hours
Difficulty: Very strenuous (due to mileage) as a day hike; moderate as an overnight back-packing trip
Highest elevation: 2,840 feet

Elevation gain: 2,350 feet
Canine compatibility: Dog friendly
Trail contact: Green Mountain Club, (802) 244-7037, www.greenmountainclub.org; Green Mountain National Forest, Manchester District, (802) 362-2307, www.fs.fed.us/r9/gmfl
Maps: USGS Danby VT Quad

Finding the trailhead: From Danby, travel south on U.S. Highway 7 for 2.0 miles. Turn left (east) on South End Road, crossing railroad tracks, and go 0.4 mile to the trailhead and parking, which are on the left side of the road.

The Hike

Baker Peak is located in the middle of the 6,720-acre Big Branch Wilderness. While Griffith Lake is not inside the designated wilderness area, it is still a pristine back-country destination. It is located in a narrow corridor between the Big Branch Wilderness and the Peru Peak Wilderness, where snowmobiling is allowed during the winter. Both early Native Americans and European settlers relied on the abundant natural resources of this region. Moose, black bear, whitetail deer, wild turkey, and beaver are common here.

Both Baker Peak and Griffith Lake make excellent hiking destinations alone, but the hike described here takes you to both in a day. The route is also perfect for an overnight if you want to break up the mileage. You can camp at the Griffith Lake tent site, then either hike Baker Peak as a diversion or hike out over the peak. The route is described as a lollipop hike, a large loop that begins and ends on the same trail.

From the trailhead, follow the sign for the Griffith Lake Trail/Baker Peak Trail (blue blazes) into the hardwoods. The Griffith Lake Trail and the Baker Peak Trail are concurrent at first. The path is wide and smooth and climbs on an easy grade parallel to McGinn Brook, which is on your left. Sign in at the registration box and then bear left, dipping over a tributary of McGinn Brook and continuing along the opposite shore.

At 0.5 mile, the trail turns left uphill, where logs block an older route, then bends to the south like an elongated switchback, eventually returning to its generally easterly direction. Moments later, a sign marks the official border of the Big Branch Wilderness.

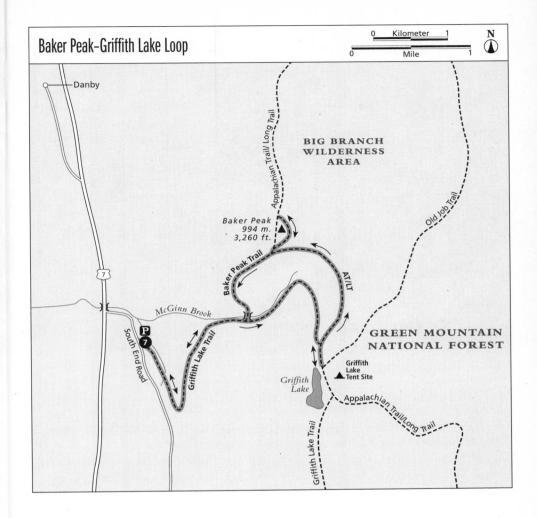

At about 1.1 miles, a footbridge aids the traverse across a section of steep side-hill slab. After the bridge, the trail seems to hang on the hillside as it rounds a rocky outcropping.

At 1.5 miles, look for a double blaze and a low rock cairn on your right, which signals a right turn onto a rougher, steeper path (no sign). Just after the turn, a short spur to a rock perch offers a nice view to the northwest. US 7 dissects the long, narrow valley below, which marks the rift between the Green Mountains and the Taconic Range. The Dorset marble quarry is to the south, and the small village of Danby lies to the north.

From here the main trail swings up the side of a shallow ravine, where you can see the cascades of McGinn Brook below through the trees. At the top of the ravine, the

View to the south from the summit of Baker Peak.

trail crosses the brook on slick moss-covered rocks. The Baker Peak Trail splits here to the left (north). Stay right on the Griffith Lake Trail, keeping the brook on your right, though the trail seems like a brook itself through this muddy area.

A short time later, the trail crosses a confluence of tributaries entering the main brook and then heads to drier ground. By 2.6 miles, the streamlets peter out. The trail bends right onto a narrower path and begins a long traverse to the southeast.

At 3.3 miles, the Griffith Lake Trail meets the Appalachian Trail/Long Trail (AT/LT; white blazes) and runs concurrent with the AT/LT–South toward the lake.

At 3.5 miles, the trail reaches the lake, which is really a large pond with a beaver dam at its north end. The Green Mountain Club maintains the tent site on the east side of the lake and charges a small overnight fee (per person) for its use during the summer and fall. Camping is only permitted at designated spots.

To continue to Baker Peak from the lake, retrace your steps heading north on the AT/LT, returning to the junction with the Griffith Lake Trail at 3.7 miles. Stay on the AT/LT–North as it travels along a plateau through more hardwoods. At 4.0 miles, the trail dips down and zigzags through a boggy area over puncheon.

At 4.3 miles, the trail passes a large boulder as it descends gradually to another short bog bridge. From here the path begins to climb, gently at first, as it meanders through the woods in a northwesterly direction.

At 5.4 miles, the AT/LT comes to a T at the Baker Peak Trail. Turn right, continuing north on the AT/LT, which is concurrent with the Baker Peak Trail to the summit of Baker Peak.

The last couple tenths of a mile is a short and steep but interesting scramble. The upper cone of Baker Peak is open rock, though it is not smooth. A metamorphic mountain, the entire summit area is a series of striated rock chunks, as if the peak were turned on its side and sliced off by some geologic force millions of years ago. It feels as though you are climbing up the back of a large scaly dragon.

The trail reaches the top of Baker Peak at 5.6 miles. A marble quarry scars the ridge to the west. The views north and south along US 7 and the Otter Creek Valley can stretch for many miles on a clear day.

From the summit, retrace your steps back to the junction where the AT/LT and Baker Peak Trail meet, at 5.8 miles. This time, continue straight through the intersection, staying on the Baker Peak Trail (blue blazes). The descent is consistent on a moderate grade down the opposite side of the ravine from the AT/LT.

At 6.7 miles, the Baker Peak Trail crosses a stream and then meets the Griffith Lake Trail, closing the loop. Bear right, continuing downhill, back around the elongated switchback, returning to the trailhead at 8.6 miles.

Miles and Directions

0.0 Start at the trailhead for the Griffith Lake Trail/Baker Peak Trail.

0.5 Cross the boundary into the Big Branch Wilderness.

1.1 Cross a footbridge over steep sidehill slab.

1.5 Turn right, then pass a rock perch with a view of the valley.

1.9 Griffith Lake Trail and Baker Peak Trail split. Bear right at the fork on the Griffith Lake Trail.

2.6 Bend right onto a narrower path and begin a long traverse to the southeast.

3.3 Head south at the junction with the AT/LT to reach the lake and the tent site.

3.5 LAKE! Return north on the AT/LT to continue to Baker Peak.

3.7 Bear right at the junction with the Griffith Lake Trail, continuing on the AT/LT-North.

4.0 Traverse a boggy area over extensive puncheon.

5.4 Turn right (north) at the T with the Baker Peak Trail. Scramble up rocks toward the summit. The Baker Peak Trail and AT/LT are concurrent here.

5.6 SUMMIT! Retrace the short distance back to the junction of the Baker Peak Trail and the AT/LT.

5.8 Continue down the Baker Peak Trail when it splits from the AT/LT.

6.7 Close the loop at the junction with the Griffith Lake Trail. Turn right (west) onto the Griffith Lake Trail, heading back toward the trailhead.

8.6 Arrive back at the trailhead.

8 Deer Leap Overlook

Short hike to a dramatic cliff with a 180–degree view of Pico Peak and the surrounding countryside.

General location: Killington
Distance: 2.2 miles out and back
Approximate hiking time: 2.0 hours
Difficulty: Moderate
Highest point: 2,670 feet
Elevation gain: 520 feet
Canine compatibility: Dog friendly, but a busy trail and no water. Dogs should be on leash around other people and at the summit cliff.
Trail contact: Green Mountain Club, (802) 244-7037, www.greenmountainclub.org; Green Mountain National Forest, Rutland Office, (802) 747-6700, www.fs.fed.us/gmfl
Maps: USGS Pico Peak Quad

Finding the trailhead: From the junction of U.S. Highways 7 and 4 in Rutland, travel 9.0 miles east on US 4. The trailhead is just past the entrance to the Pico Peak Ski Area at the top of Sherburne Pass. Park in the large dirt lot on the south side of the road. Carefully cross the road to the trailhead, which leaves from the right (east) side of the Inn at Long Trail. If approaching from the east, from the junction where US 4 and Route 100 North split near the main entrance to the Killington Resort, continue 1.6 miles west on US 4 to the top of Sherburne Pass.

Deer Leap Overlook.

Deer Leap Overlook

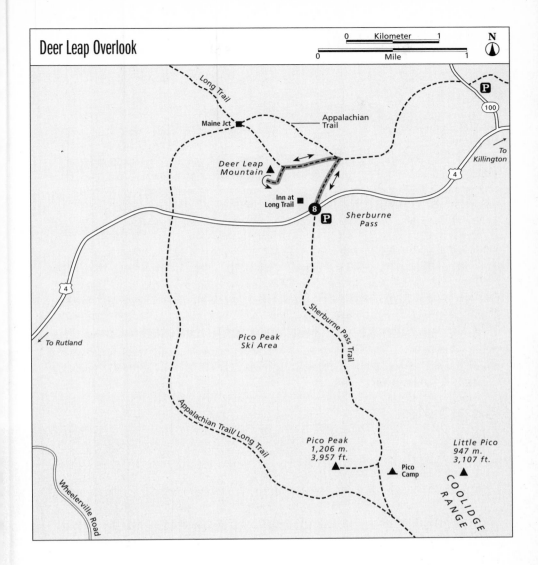

The Hike

Deer Leap Overlook, also known as Dear Leap Cliff and Deer Leap Lookout, is a cliffy shoulder of Deer Leap Mountain. It is a popular perch with a stunning view of Pico Peak directly across Sherburne Pass. It towers above US 4, gleaming bright white from the high amount of quartz in the granite. The hike passes just east of "Maine Junction," the point where after 105 miles together, the Appalachian Trail (AT) and Long Trail (LT) split, with the AT turning east toward New Hampshire and the LT continuing north toward Canada.

At the trailhead, sign in at the box, then follow the Sherburne Trail (blue blazes) into the woods. At first, the well-used trail climbs moderately, heading east parallel to US 4, away from your cliff-top destination. The trail is initially rocky and rough.

At about 0.2 mile, the trail dips downhill and then levels off. The footing becomes smoother.

At 0.3 mile, the trail bends away from the road, climbing steadily. Be careful to stay on the trail and off the unofficial shortcuts in this section to help reduce human impact.

At 0.5 mile, the trail bends to the right (east) and ends abruptly at the Appalachian Trail. Turn left onto the AT South (white blazes), though you are actually heading north briefly.

About 200 feet later, the AT comes to the junction with the Deer Leap Overlook Trail (blue blazes). Turn left (northwest) onto the Dear Leap Overlook Trail. The climb is steady at first, then becomes steeper until it crests a short ridge. Here the flora changes abruptly to white birches and evergreens. The trail levels off and then descends slightly as it crosses the ridge.

The path traverses a muddy area over several puncheon and then reaches the junction with the spur to Deer Leap Overlook at 0.9 mile. Bear left at this junction, taking the higher path to stay on the ridge.

At 1.1 miles, the trail dips sharply, then winds downhill briefly over a narrow board-walk to the lookout. The open rock knob is a perfect for spot for a picnic. Pico Peak dominates the view to the south, though you can also see the hills to the east and west.

Return by the same route.

Miles and Directions

0.0   Start at the trailhead for the Sherburne Pass Trail. Begin climbing, heading east, parallel to US 4.

0.3   Bend left, away from US 4, climbing steadily.

0.5   Turn left on the AT South. After 200 feet, turn left (northwest) onto the Dear Leap Overlook Trail.

0.9   Bear left onto the spur trail to Dear Leap Overlook. Dip down and then cross the narrow boardwalk.

1.1   OVERLOOK! Return to the trailhead by the same route.

2.2   Arrive back at the trailhead.

9 Killington Peak via the Bucklin Trail

Hike to the rocky summit of the second-highest peak in Vermont. Numerous wild-flowers in early summer; optional overnight at Cooper Lodge (cabin); spectacular view, particularly to the north along the spine of the Green Mountains.

General location: Mendon
Distance: 7.2 miles out and back
Approximate hiking time: 6 hours
Difficulty: Very strenuous (due to elevation gain)
Highest elevation: 4,241 feet

Elevation gain: 2,480 feet
Canine compatibility: Dog friendly
Trail contact: Green Mountain Club, (802) 244-7037, www.greenmountainclub.org
Map: USGS Killington Peak Quad

Finding the trailhead: From Rutland, take U.S. Highway 4 east for 5.0 miles. Turn right (south) on Wheelerville Road (dirt). Continue 4.0 miles, passing the Rutland Watershed Area on your left. Just after a 90-degree bend in the road, look for the trailhead on the left.

Hiker approaching the summit of Killington Peak with its old fire tower.

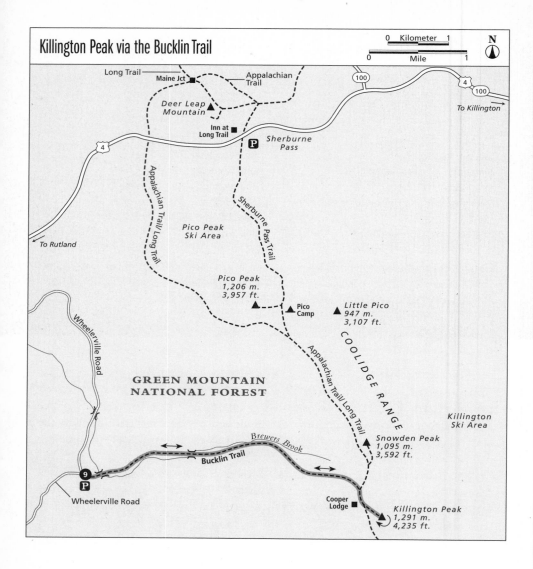

Killington Peak via the Bucklin Trail

Map labels:

Long Trail — Maine Jct — Appalachian Trail — 100

Deer Leap Mountain

Inn at Long Trail — Sherburne Pass — P — 4 — 100 — To Killington

Appalachian Trail/Long Trail

Sherburne Pass Trail

Pico Peak Ski Area

To Rutland

Pico Peak 1,206 m. 3,957 ft.

Pico Camp

Little Pico 947 m. 3,107 ft.

COOLIDGE RANGE

Wheelerville Road

GREEN MOUNTAIN NATIONAL FOREST

Appalachian Trail/Long Trail

Killington Ski Area

Brewers Brook

Bucklin Trail

Snowden Peak 1,095 m. 3,592 ft.

9 — P

Wheelerville Road

Cooper Lodge

Killington Peak 1,291 m. 4,235 ft.

N

The Hike

Killington Peak is the highest of the six peaks that make up the Killington ski resort and one of only five summits with elevations over 4,000 feet in Vermont. There are four ways to climb this towering peak, from the north and from the south along the Appalachian Trail/Long Trail (AT/LT), from the east up one of the ski area's interpretive hiking trails, and from the west via the Bucklin Trail. The Bucklin Trail, described here, is a shorter route than either approach on the AT/LT and offers a truer backcountry experience than the routes up the ski area side.

Cooper Lodge en route to Killington Peak.

From the trailhead, the Bucklin Trail (blue blazes) enters the woods on an old woods road that is also part of the Catamount Trail, a winter-use trail for Nordic skiing and snowshoeing. The Catamount Trail system winds 300 miles through the state and is marked with small blue plastic diamonds. Ignore them and instead follow the blue painted rectangles, the universal blaze for an access trail to the AT/LT, which is marked with white rectangles.

The Bucklin Trail immediately crosses Brewers Brook over a footbridge and then follows the brook, gradually rising away from it. The trail narrows to a footpath through a plethora of wildflowers in early summer, including clover, daisy, buttercup, wild rose, and devil's paintbrush.

At 0.8 mile, the trail recrosses Brewers Brook on a substantial bridge. It continues up the other side of the brook, again distancing itself from the water.

At 1.8 miles, the Bucklin Trail comes to a junction with an unnamed route used for evacuating injured backcountry skiers during the winter. The evacuation route is blocked by a low dirt berm. Bear right, heading uphill. The trail becomes steeper now, though the footing remains smooth. When a ridge line first appears through the tree tops, look for an unusual twisted tree next to the trail. It is about 3 feet in diameter and has a huge hollow in its uphill side that is big enough to stand in.

The trail flattens out briefly as you enter the subalpine zone, where coniferous trees take over. At 3.4 miles, the Bucklin Trail reaches the AT/LT. Continue uphill on the AT/LT–South. From here on, more roots crisscross the trail, though the ascent is easier.

At the next fork, a sign points right to a water source, but turn left to reach Cooper Lodge at 3.5 miles. Cooper Lodge is one of many cabins maintained by the Green Mountain Club (GMC) along the Long Trail. Constructed of stone and wood, the lodge is relatively spacious, with sleeping platforms that hold up to sixteen people and a full-size picnic table inside it. The entire northwestern side of the cabin has windows, redefining the cliché "a room with a view."

Cooper Lodge was built in 1939 by the Vermont Forest Service. It is located on state land that was donated by Mortimer R. Proctor, a former president of the GMC and governor of Vermont. Proctor made the donation in honor of Charles P. Cooper, another former president of the club. The GMC is considering removal of this shelter, which is the object of frequent vandalism and abuse due to its easy access from the ski area, so backpackers should check with the GMC first before assuming they will find shelter here. A GMC ridge runner may collect a small, per-person fee for overnight use of the lodge. If Cooper Lodge is full, bear right, up the log steps, to find a number of tent platforms in the woods just above the cabin.

From here the climb to the summit is short but steep and rocky. The rocks feel like steps prepared for giants rather than humans.

At 3.6 miles, the trail arrives at the summit. While not expansive, it is bare and well worth the climb, particularly for the view to the north, where you can see Mount Mansfield along the spine of Vermont's highest peaks. Blue Mountain lies to the left of Pico Peak by Chittenden Reservoir. Tree-covered Little Killington lies to the west in the foreground, with Bald Mountain and the Rutland Valley farther away. On a clear day, look through the gap on the far side of Rutland to see the Adirondacks. To catch Mount Ascutney to the southeast, you have to look through the jumble of communication equipment on an old fire tower, which is not open to the public. The rocky trail beyond the summit leads to the Killington gondola only 200 yards away. On weekends, many people ride up the gondola and then make the short hike from there to the summit. It is best to save this trek for midweek if you want this popular peak to yourself.

Return by the same route.

Miles and Directions

0.0   Start at the trailhead for the Bucklin Trail, concurrent with the Catamount Trail. Immediately cross Brewers Brook on a footbridge.

0.8   Recross Brewers Brook on another bridge.

1.8   Junction with backcountry-skiing evacuation trail. Turn right heading uphill.

3.4   Junction with the AT/LT. Take the AT/LT-South to reach Killington Peak.

3.5   Visit Cooper Lodge.

3.6   SUMMIT! Return by the same route.

7.2   Arrive back at the trailhead.

10 Little Rock Pond and Green Mountain via the Homer Stone Brook Trail

A little bit of everything—a cascading brook, a large secluded pond, and mountain views—makes this a perfect day trip or an easy overnighter.

General location: South Wallingford
Distance: 7.1-mile out and back with a loop around the pond
Approximate hiking time: 6 hours
Difficulty: More challenging
Highest point: Green Mountain, 2,509 feet
Elevation gain: 1,210 feet to Little Rock Pond, plus 660 feet to summit of Green Mountain
Canine compatibility: Dog friendly, though dogs should be on leash near ledges on Green Mountain and on the cliff above the pond. There is one difficult rock for inexperienced dogs on the ascent up Green Mountain.
Trail contact: Green Mountain Club, (802) 244-7037, www.greenmountainclub.org; Green Mountain National Forest, Rutland Office, (802) 747-6700, www.fs.fed.us/gmfl
Maps: USGS Wallingford Quad

Finding the trailhead: In South Wallingford, turn east on Hartsboro Road, crossing over a small bridge and railroad tracks. At 0.1 mile, bear right (south) on Homer Stone Road. Go 0.3 mile to the trailhead on the left (east) side of the road. Park in the small grassy area by the trail sign.

The Hike

Most people (and other guidebooks) approach Little Rock Pond via the Appalachian Trail/Long Trail (AT/LT) from USFS Road 10 south of the pond. The Homer Stone Brook Trail (blue blazes) is 0.3-mile longer, round-trip, but it is a perfect 10 as far as hiking in southern Vermont goes. It begins with an easy walk through the woods that nips away at the elevation as it follows scenic Homer Stone Brook, paralleling the brook most of the way to the pond—a small lake really. Once at the pond, you can explore the loop around it, make the short climb up Green Mountain on its western shore, or both. The route described here takes you on the entire trek.

The Homer Stone Brook Trail begins as a smooth woods road, climbing and easily up a hillside through a young hardwood forest. At about 0.2 mile, the trail crosses the second of two stone walls, arriving at an unnamed junction with another woods road. Turn right, heading uphill.

At 0.3 mile, bear right (south) at the fork, following the blue arrow and still climbing easily. The trail soon becomes more persistent as it heads upward through a stand of mature conifers and white birches.

At 0.6 mile, you can hear Homer Stone Brook to your right. The trails levels off as it comes to a fork. Bear right (east), staying above the brook. Around the next bend, the brook is suddenly adjacent to the path on your right. Above this point, the ascent mellows, sometimes climbing next to the brook and sometimes high above it.

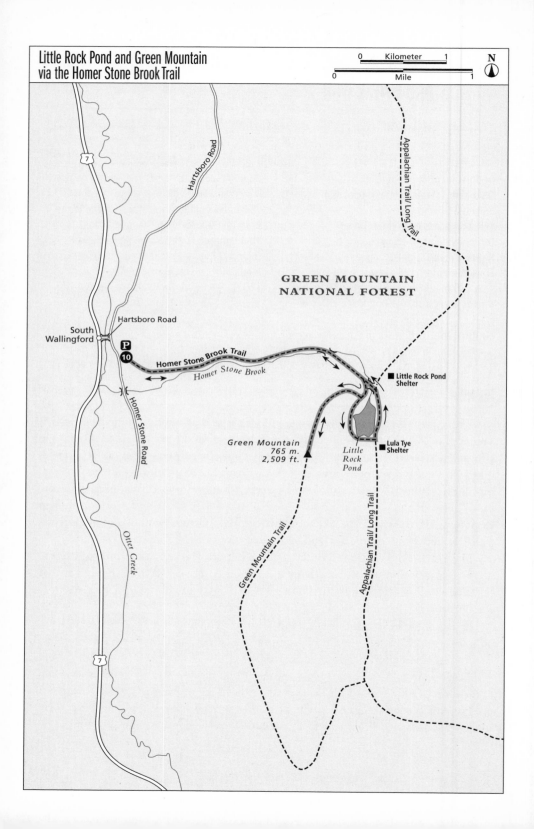

Little Rock Pond and Green Mountain via the Homer Stone Brook Trail

0 — Kilometer — 1

0 — Mile — 1

N

Hartsboro Road

7

Appalachian Trail/Long Trail

GREEN MOUNTAIN
NATIONAL FOREST

Hartsboro Road

South
Wallingford

P
10

Homer Stone Brook Trail

Homer Stone Brook

Homer Stone Road

Little Rock Pond
Shelter

Green Mountain
765 m.
2,509 ft.

Little
Rock
Pond

Lula Tye
Shelter

Otter Creek

Green Mountain Trail

Appalachian Trail/Long Trail

7

At 1.5 miles, the trail levels off and comes to a junction with another woods road. Turn right (south), crossing the brook on stepping stones. (*Note:* This can be a wet crossing during spring runoff or after heavy rain.) The trail immediately forks on the opposite side of the stream. Bear right (west), go 30 yards, and then turn left (south) at the blue arrow. At the top of the short rise, there is yet another junction. Turn left (east) and begin a steadier climb.

The trail remains wide but is now rockier and more eroded. It angles away from the brook on a noticeably steeper ascent until you reach Little Rock Pond and the end of the Homer Stone Brook Trail at 2.3 miles.

Turn right, following the western shoreline on the Green Mountain/Little Rock Pond Loop Trail (blue blazes), a narrower and lesser-used footpath than the AT/LT, which runs along the eastern shoreline. At about 2.4 miles, the trail bends away from the pond to a junction where the mountain trail and the pond loop split. To climb Green Mountain, bear right (north) on the Green Mountain Trail.

The Green Mountain Trail winds uphill, then levels off on a shoulder of the mountain. It dips slightly on a short traverse to the south and then bends to the west, ascending steadily to the summit ridge. At about 2.9 miles, the trail passes an interesting rib of rock protruding from the mountainside, as if a giant serpent were buried there and all that can be seen aboveground is its back.

Above the rock spine, the trail takes a sharp bend to the left (south). The trees turn coniferous, and the forest path gives way more and more to rock slab and ledge. After a short scramble up a 10-foot rock "wall" (follow the crack in the rock for the easiest route), the trail reaches the summit ridge. There are several rock perches en route to the true summit at 3.3 miles. For the best view, follow the pond view sign at the summit to a short spur across more open ledge. At the end of the spur, you can glimpse the southern end of the pond far below, though the panorama to the south is more impressive down the long Otter Creek Valley.

Retrace your steps down the Green Mountain Trail, arriving back at the pond at 4.2 miles. Turn right (south) at the pond, following the Little Rock Pond Loop. The loop passes over an impressive 40-foot cliff above the pond, where there are excellent views of the entire pond and its lone island.

At 4.5 miles, the Little Rock Pond Loop ends at a T with the AT/LT (white blazes). Turn left and follow the AT/LT–North to close the loop around the pond. The trail immediately passes the Lula Tye tent site and the short spur trail that leads to an eight-person shelter. The shelter and tent site are maintained by the Green Mountain Club and named for a woman who worked for the club for twenty-nine years during the first half of the twentieth century.

The AT/LT traverses the eastern shore of the pond. At 4.7 miles, at the opposite end of the pond, it passes a second tent site and a spur to the Little Rock Pond shelter, another eight-person shelter that is also maintained by the Green Mountain Club. A caretaker oversees both shelters and tent sites during the summer, collecting a small usage fee from those who wish to camp there on a first-come, first-served basis.

A boy resting on a cliff above Little Rock Pond.

At the Little Rock Pond tent site, the trail takes a sharp turn away from the pond to go around a small backwater, then arrives at the junction with the Green Mountain Trail. Bear left (west) on the Green Mountain Trail. The path immediately crosses a bridge over a beaver dam at the outlet to the pond, which is also the top (source) of Homer Stone Brook, closing the loop around the pond at 4.8 miles.

Retrace your steps back down the Homer Stone Brook Trail, returning to the trailhead at 7.1 miles.

Miles and Directions

0.0 Start at the trailhead for the Homer Stone Brook Trail.

0.2 Cross a stone wall at the four-way junction. Turn right, up the hill.

0.3 Bear right at the blue arrow, climbing through tall conifers and white birches.

0.6 Bear right at the fork. Come alongside Homer Stone Brook around the next bend in the trail.

1.5 Turn right, crossing the brook.

2.3 Homer Stone Brook Trail ends at Little Rock Pond. Turn right on the Green Mountain/Little Rock Pond Loop Trail along western shore of the pond.

2.4 Turn right on the Green Mountain Trail away from the pond.

2.9 Pass a rock spine. Climb rock slab and ledges to Green Mountain's summit ridge.

3.3 Arrive at summit of Green Mountain. Follow short POND VIEW spur for the best view of the pond and the Otter Creek Valley. Retrace your steps back to the pond.

4.2 Arrive back at the shoreline. Turn right on the Little Rock Pond Loop, continuing along the western shore of the pond and passing over a 40-foot cliff.

4.5 Turn left on the AT/LT–North, passing the Lula Tye tent site.

4.7 Pass the Little Rock Pond tent site. Turn sharply away from the pond to avoid a small backwater.

4.8 Cross a bridge over the beaver dam and pond outlet, closing the pond loop. Turn right on the Homer Stone Brook Trail and retrace your steps back to the trailhead.

7.1 Arrive back at the trailhead.

TERMS OF THE TRAIL

There are a number of terms used to describe the trails and certain geologic features in the Green Mountains that might differ from other regions in the United States. Here's a list of the more common ones used in this book and their meanings:

Blaze: A trail marker, usually a rectangle painted vertically on a sturdy tree or rock.

Brook: Larger than a stream, but smaller than an official river. Brooks in Vermont are named corridors of water that resemble small rivers in size and water flow.

Lodge: A rustic mountain cabin maintained by the Green Mountain Club along the LT, available to backpackers on a first-come, first-served basis. Also called a "camp."

Notch: A distinct narrow passage through the mountains, also called a "gap" or a "pass."

Puncheon: A narrow, low footbridge, usually two boards or two logs wide, that raises hikers just above the mud. Also called "bog bridges" and "duck boards."

Ridge runner: A member of the Green Mountain Club stationed atop mountains with alpine zones who educates hikers on low-impact backcountry travel while monitoring the health of the fragile flora.

Spur: A short unnamed side trail that ends at a specific destination, such as a cliff-top view or the side of a stream.

Stream: A corridor of water, usually unnamed, smaller than a brook. Many streams in the Green Mountains dry up by mid-summer.

Streamlet: A small unreliable stream.

Woods road: A wide section of trail, for foot travel only, that was formerly a logging road or dirt road.

11 Okemo Mountain via the Healdville Trail

A pleasant hike through an airy hardwood forest along a cascading brook to a historic fire tower with a 360-degree view.

General location: Mount Holly
Distance: 5.8 miles out and back
Approximate hiking time: 4.5 hours
Difficulty: More challenging
Highest elevation: 3,343 feet
Elevation gain: 1,943 feet
Canine compatibility: Dog friendly. Do not

take your dog up the fire tower!
Trail contact: Okemo State Forest, (802) 885-8855; Vermont Department of Forests, Parks and Recreation, (802) 886-2215, www .vtstateparks.com
Maps: USGS Mount Holly Quad

Finding the trailhead: From the main entrance to the Okemo Mountain Resort in Ludlow, travel 4.0 miles north on Route 103. Turn left onto Station Road. After crossing the railroad tracks, look for the parking lot and the trailhead on the left.

The Hike

The Green Mountain Club recommends staying off the Long Trail during mud season to protect it from excessive erosion, which makes Okemo Mountain, also called Ludlow Mountain, a particularly good choice if you have the urge to hike before Memorial Day. The Healdville Trail (blue blazes), which is the main hiking trail up Okemo Mountain, is neither steep nor overly wet. It is located on the northern side of the mountain away from the ski area, so it feels like a true backcountry experience.

The origin of the name *Okemo* is unclear. Historians prefer the Chippewa translation, "chieftain," to the Abenaki translation, "louse." The origin of the name *Ludlow* is for a Viscount Ludlow, a wealthy English lord during the 1700s, or perhaps for his namesake town in Shropshire, where it means "hill by the rapid river." In the case of Ludlow Mountain, the Black River flows past its base, making "Ludlow" a fitting name for the mountain as well. Take your pick.

Though now maintained by the State of Vermont as part of the 7,327-acre Okemo State Forest, the Healdville Trail was originally built by the Vermont Youth Conservation Corps (VYCC). Formed in 1985, the VYCC hires young people, ages sixteen to twenty-four, to work on conservation projects throughout the state, such as building and maintaining hiking trails on state land.

The Healdville Trail is certainly well-maintained, with real footbridges rather than two old logs anchored in place. It starts over the first of these bridges before heading into a hardwood forest. The footing is easy, and the trail is wide. It quickly crosses another stream and then begins to climb steadily along the left side of Branch Brook. The brook tumbles over a number of small waterfalls, forming a series of tiny pools, each a perfect place to soak your feet.

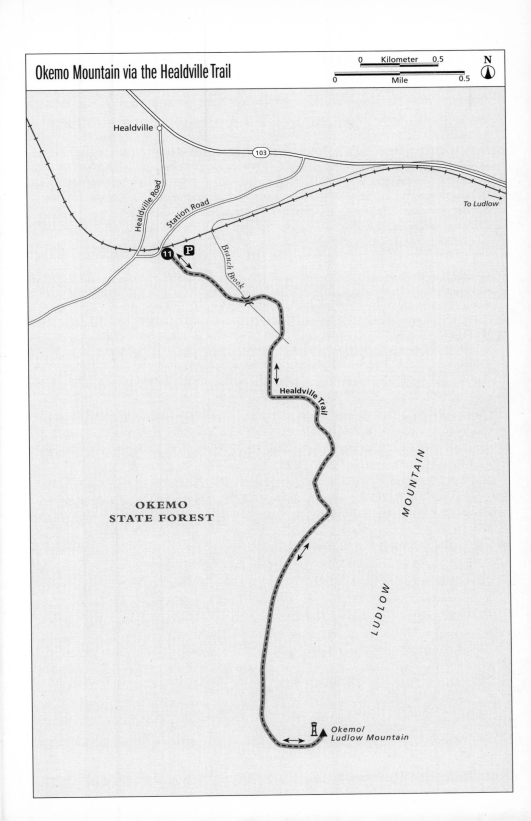

Okemo Mountain via the Healdville Trail

Kilometer

Mile

N

Healdville

103

To Ludlow

Healdville Road

Station Road

11 P

Branch Brook

Healdville Trail

MOUNTAIN

OKEMO
STATE FOREST

LUDLOW

Okemol
Ludlow Mountain

At 1.5 miles, the trail bends right and begins a long traverse to the south. At 1.9 miles, it passes a sign that reads HEALDVILLE TRAIL. An unnamed side trail departs the Healdville Trail to the left (uphill) of the sign. Go straight, staying on the main trail.

The path dips down over a clear, rocky stream and then continues to climb. Just below the summit, it passes a stone chimney and the stone outline of the former fire-watcher's cabin, then comes to the intersection with a trail leading to the Mountain Road parking lot. Turn right to reach the fire tower at 2.9 miles.

Though slightly higher than the top of the ski area, the summit of Okemo is below tree line. However, the 55-foot fire tower lifts you into the sky above the tree-tops, permitting an impressive 360-degree view. Mount Washington and the White Mountains lie to the northeast. Mount Ascutney is closer and south of the Whites. Mount Monadnock is in the distance beyond the chairlift terminal. From the other side of the tower (opposite the ski area), you can see a significant part of the main ridge of the Green Mountains to the west.

Return by the same route.

Miles and Directions

0.0 Start at the trailhead for the Healdville Trail. Head into the hardwoods over a well-constructed footbridge.

1.5 Bend to the right and begin a long traverse to the south.

1.9 Pass the HEALDVILLE TRAIL sign, ignoring the smaller side trail.

2.7 Pass the remains of the former fire-watcher's cabin.

2.9 SUMMIT! Climb the fire tower for a 360-degree view and then return by the same route.

5.8 Arrive back at the trailhead.

◀ *Remains of the old firewatcher's cabin on Okemo Mountain.*

12 Pico Peak via the Sherburne Trail

A steady climb that passes a cave and ascends through two climate zones—northern hardwood forest and boreal forest—to a small hut with a huge view to the north and south.

General location: Killington
Distance: 5.8 miles out and back
Approximate hiking time: 4.5 hours
Difficulty: More challenging
Highest elevation: 3,957 feet
Elevation gain: 1,807 feet

Canine compatibility: Dog friendly
Trail contact: Green Mountain Club, (802) 244-7037, www.greenmountainclub.org; Green Mountain National Forest, Rochester District, (802) 767-4261, www.fs.fed.us/r9/gmfl
Map: USGS Pico Peak Quad

Finding the trailhead: From Rutland, take U.S. Highway 4 west for 9.0 miles to the top of Sherburne Pass, just west of the entrance to the Pico Peak Ski Area. The trailhead begins at the end of the parking lot on the south side of the road, across the street from the Inn at Long Trail. If approaching from the east, from the junction where US 4 and Route 100 North split near the main entrance to Killington Resort, continue 1.6 miles west on US 4 to the top of Sherburne Pass.

The Hike

The Sherburne Trail (blue blazes) was originally a section of the Appalachian Trail/ Long Trail (AT/LT) and dates back to 1913, when the Long Trail was first cut. In the 1990s the AT/LT was relocated slightly west of the Sherburne Trail to allow for a potential ski area expansion. The expansion did not happen, but the relocation of the AT/LT remains, which is a good thing if your goal is to hike to the top of Pico Peak. While still a popular hike, it is quieter than it used to be now that through-hikers on the AT/LT take the newer trail.

From the sign-in box, the Sherburne Trail starts climbing moderately through a hardwood forest. A fertile mix of ferns, low leafy shrubs, wood sorrel, and grasses grow along the edges of this well-worn trail. The footing varies from rocks and roots to sections of slab. Ignore the first unmarked but obvious spur to the right. It leads to a ski area work road with no view.

At 1.3 miles, the trail passes two sinkholes on the right. The first is smaller, about 7 feet deep. The second is twice that size, with two short unofficial footpaths leading into it. A stream also flows into the larger hole, disappearing into the earth. Avoid exploring the sinkholes. The soil can be unstable around them, and both are part of a small cave, which is unsafe for novice spelunking.

Above the sinkholes, the trail climbs gradually, crossing a small streamlet, and then turns toward the west, gaining noticeable altitude. Eventually, it swings back to the south as the trees become predominantly evergreen. It turns to the west again, then continues on a long, shallow ascent to a junction with the Summit Glades ski

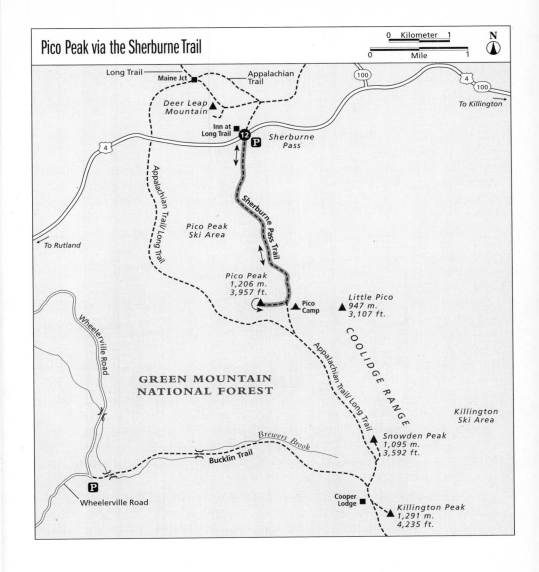

Pico Peak via the Sherburne Trail

0 Kilometer 1
0 Mile 1

N

Long Trail
Maine Jct
Appalachian Trail

Deer Leap
Mountain

Inn at
Long Trail

12 P

Sherburne
Pass

To Killington

To Rutland

Appalachian Trail/Long Trail

Sherburne Pass Trail

Pico Peak
Ski Area

Pico Peak
1,206 m.
3,957 ft.

Pico
Camp

Little Pico
947 m.
3,107 ft.

Wheelerville Road

GREEN MOUNTAIN
NATIONAL FOREST

Appalachian Trail/Long Trail

C O O L I D G E   R A N G E

Killington
Ski Area

Brewers Brook

Bucklin Trail

Snowden Peak
1,095 m.
3,592 ft.

P
Wheelerville Road

Cooper
Lodge

Killington Peak
1,291 m.
4,235 ft.

trail (no sign). From the ski trail, you get a lengthy view to the north past Deer Leap Overlook and the Chittenden Reservoir and on to some of the higher peaks in the Green Mountain chain.

After 20 paces, the Sherburne Trail reenters the woods on the left, marked by only a blue blaze (no sign). At this point, you have two choices: take the steeper ski trail or the flatter footpath to the summit. Opting for the footpath, turn left and then continue along the now-flat trail. Just after a small spring, marked by a white pipe poking out of the hillside, the trail reaches Pico Shelter, also called Pico Camp, at 2.5 miles.

Pico Shelter is an excellent place to sleep if you are backpacking. It has rough bunks, a table, and a nice view of Killington Peak. *Note:* Campfires are not allowed in the Coolidge Range (Killington and Pico region). The shelter is available on a first-come, first-served basis. A ridge runner from the Green Mountain Club stays here and may collect the small overnight fee. If the shelter is full, you may not tent-camp by the shelter. The overflow camping area is 0.3 mile away on a nearby ski trail.

For the final climb to the summit, turn right, passing the entrance to the shelter, onto the Pico Link Trail (blue blazes). The trail climbs steeply past the back of the shelter to another ski trail. At the junction with the ski trail, look left for a more expansive view of Killington Peak.

Cross the ski trail and reenter the woods by a small rock cairn. The trail continues to climb steeply to a gravel work road. Turn left, heading up the road for a few paces, and then turn right through a strip of trees onto yet another ski trail, called Forty-Niner (no sign). Turn left, continuing uphill on Forty-Niner toward the communication towers on the summit.

Just below the summit, at 2.8 miles, the trail comes to the Warming Hut and the top of a chairlift. The Warming Hut is open year-round. In the winter, it serves skiers as a first-aid and information cabin. In the summer, it is empty. The small deck on the front of the hut is a perfect picnic spot, with built-in benches around its railing. The views of nearby Killington to the south and Ascutney, the pointed peak with ski trails farther to the southeast, are spectacular. Looking past the lift terminal to the north, the layers of peaks include Mount Abraham, Mount Ellen, and even Mount Mansfield on a clear day.

For a view to the west, you need to hike slightly farther to the true summit of the mountain at 2.9 miles. However, the summit is a jumble of work roads, maintenance buildings, lift terminals, and communication towers. It is worth a quick glance, but the Warming Hut offers the serenity that most hikers seek on a mountaintop. *Note:* Always stay clear of the chairlifts, as the lifts can turn any time, even in summer.

Return by the same route.

Miles and Directions

0.0 Start at the trailhead for the Sherburne Trail. Climbs moderately at first through a lush hardwood forest.

1.3 Pass a sinkhole and then a larger one beside the trail.

2.5 Turn right at Pico Shelter, also called Pico Camp, onto the Pico Link Trail, heading uphill.

2.8 Have a picnic and take in the views to the north, east, and south at the Warming Hut.

2.9 SUMMIT! Best spot for a view to the west. Return by the same route.

5.8 Arrive back at the trailhead.

◀ *The view from the upper trail on Pico Peak.*

13 White Rocks Cliffs via the Keewaydin Trail

A relatively short hike to a dramatic cliff that passes a cascading waterfall on Bully Brook and some unusual rock cairns along the way.

General location: Wallingford
Distance: 3.2 miles out and back (including detour to Bully Brook)
Approximate hiking time: 3 hours
Difficulty: Moderate
Highest elevation: 2,400 feet
Elevation gain: 1,150 feet
Canine compatibility: Dog friendly. Dogs should be on leash around the picnic area at the trailhead and by the cliff.

Trail contact: Green Mountain Club, (802) 244-7037, www.greenmountainclub.org; Green Mountain National Forest, Manchester District, (802) 362-2307, www.fs.fed.us/r9/gmfl
Maps: USGS Wallingford Quad
Special considerations: Before going on this hike, check with the Green Mountain National Forest office. The cliffs may be closed from early spring through mid-August if peregrine falcons are nesting here.

Finding the trailhead: From Route 140 between Wallingford and East Wallingford, turn southeast onto Sugar Hill Road. Take the first right onto White Rocks Picnic Road and park at the picnic area. The trailhead is at the far end of the parking lot by the USDA Forest Service notice board. (The trailhead for the White Rocks Ice Beds also leaves from this parking lot.) The picnic-area gate is open from 6:00 a.m. to 10:00 p.m. No overnight camping. **Note:** Though this hike can also be done entirely on the Appalachian Trail/Long Trail (AT/LT), which crosses Route 140 east of Sugar Hill Road, there is no trailhead parking. As Route 140 is narrow with many blind turns, this is not a recommended access point for this hike.

The Hike

From the parking lot, the Keewaydin Trail (blue blazes) seems more like a forest road than a footpath. It is wide and flat at first, but soon begins to ascend moderately and then rather steeply. The footing is smooth, which makes the climb easier as it angles up the hillside above Bully Brook.

At 0.2 mile, a spur to the left gives a view of Bully Brook's cascades through the trees. The forest is healthy and lush around you. From here the trail becomes rockier and then crosses a stream just before joining the AT/LT at 0.4 mile.

To visit Bully Brook, turn left on the AT/LT–North (white blazes) and go a short way to a spur trail down to the cascades. To continue to the cliffs, turn right onto the AT/LT–South.

The trail becomes smooth again, climbing steeply through hardwoods. At 1.0 mile, the spur to Greenwall Shelter departs to the left as the trail bends sharply right. It then meanders through the forest on a more moderate grade.

At 1.4 miles, the White Rocks Cliffs Trail (blue blazes) departs to the right. The junction is hard to miss. It is cluttered with small, odd rock formations reminiscent of

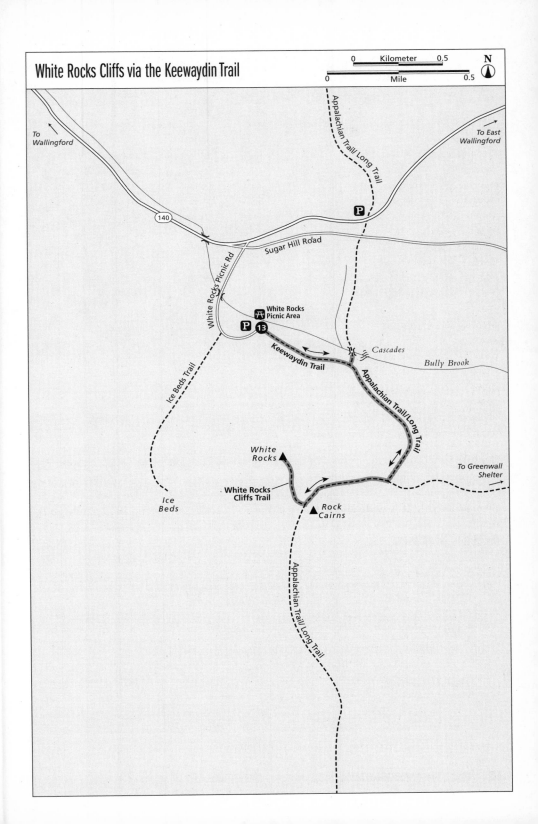

White Rocks Cliffs via the Keewaydin Trail

0   Kilometer   0.5

0   Mile   0.5

N

To Wallingford

To East Wallingford

Appalachian Trail/ Long Trail

140

Sugar Hill Road

White Rocks Picnic Rd

White Rocks Picnic Area

13

Keewaydin Trail

Cascades

Bully Brook

Ice Beds Trail

Appalachian Trail/Long Trail

To Greenwall Shelter

White Rocks

White Rocks Cliffs Trail

Ice Beds

Rock Cairns

Appalachian Trail/Long Trail

Another hiker contributing to the "cairn art" above White Rocks Cliff.

Dr. Seuss. Various hikers have created this "cairn art" by stacking small rocks to look like mini-towers and other intriguing shapes.

Turn right onto the White Rocks Cliffs Trail, which descends gently before coming to a clearing atop the cliff at 1.6 miles. The drop is almost 1,000 feet to the valley floor. If you head to the right through the scrubby trees, the view is eye-popping, including the Otter Creek Valley, the Taconic Range, and even the Adirondacks in New York.

Return by the same route.

Miles and Directions

0.0 Start at the trailhead for the Keeywadin Trail, a wide forest road.

0.4 Turn left at the junction with the AT/LT, heading north. Descend a short way to see Bully Brook, then return to the junction and follow the AT/LT–South.

1.0 Pass the spur to Greenwall Shelter. Stay on the AT/LT–South, which bends sharply to the right.

1.4 Turn right onto the White Rocks Cliffs Trail as you pass through cairn art.

1.6 CLIFF! Bear right through the brush and scrubby trees to get the best view, and then return by the same route.

3.2 Arrive back at the trailhead.

14 White Rocks Ice Beds

A short hike to a mountainside boulder field that gives off cool air throughout the summer.

General location: Wallingford
Distance: 1.8 miles out and back
Approximate hiking time: 2 hours
Difficulty: Easy
Highest elevation: 1,400 feet
Elevation gain: 440 feet
Canine compatibility: Not dog friendly due to vertical boulder field at your destination.

Trail contact: Green Mountain National Forest, Manchester District, (802) 362-2307, www.fs.fed.us/r9/gmfl
Maps: USGS Wallingford Quad
Special considerations: The picnic area gate is open from 6:00 a.m. to 10:00 p.m. No overnight camping.

Finding the trailhead: From Route 140 between Wallingford and East Wallingford, turn southeast onto Sugar Hill Road. Take the first right onto White Rocks Picnic Road and park at the picnic area. The trailhead is on the right as you enter the parking lot. (The trailhead for White Rocks Cliffs also leaves from this parking lot.)

The Hike

Looking for a cool hike on a hot day? This one is cool both figuratively and literally. It goes to the base of an enormous boulder pile, which was likely formed during the last ice age. The rocks are Cheshire quartzite, which gives them a white appearance. During the winter, ice accumulates within the deep, sheltered spaces between the boulders and lasts well into August.

From the parking lot, enter the woods on the Ice Beds Trail (blue blazes) over a couple of footbridges. The wide, rooted path immediately heads up over rocks and soon runs parallel to a cliff. It bends right behind a rocky outcropping that marks the edge of the cliff. Several spurs take you to the edge, though they are narrow and rough and can be treacherous. Have patience. At 0.3 mile, the main trail reaches White Rocks Overlook, which offers an even better view of the peak and rock slide across the narrow ravine.

From here the footing alternates from smooth slab to scattered rocks and dirt. There is little undergrowth among the tall spruce trees, only moss, as you continue to parallel the cliff. At 0.5 mile, the trail dips and then bends right, heading downhill, but take a few more steps straight ahead to another vista. This time the view extends across the hills to the west.

At the bottom of a short, steep hill, the trail bends left (west), traverses through the woods, and then continues downhill through a couple of short switchbacks until it levels off again. The footing is soft and smooth.

At 0.7 mile, the trail reaches a fork. Bear left, heading downhill toward the brook,

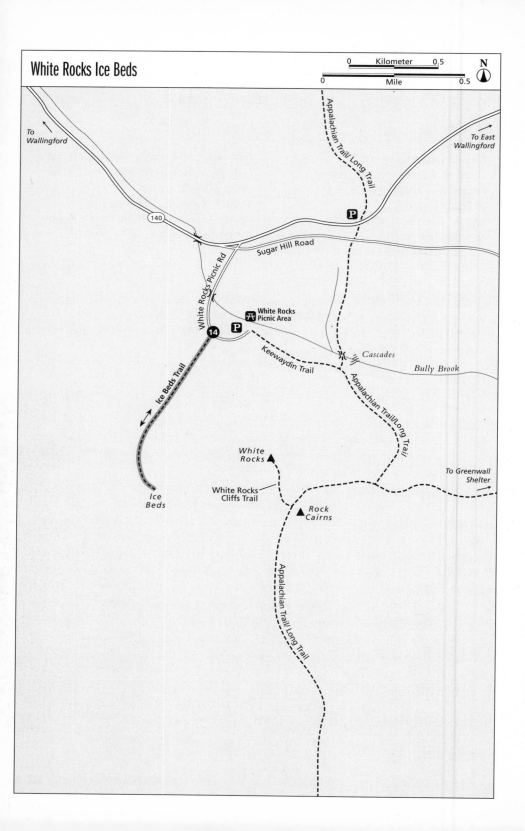

White Rocks Ice Beds

0 Kilometer 0.5
0 Mile 0.5

N

To Wallingford

Appalachian Trail/Long Trail

To East Wallingford

140

White Rocks Picnic Rd

Sugar Hill Road

P

White Rocks Picnic Area

P

14

Keewaydin Trail

Cascades

Bully Brook

Ice Beds Trail

Appalachian Trail/Long Trail

Ice Beds

White Rocks

White Rocks Cliffs Trail

Rock Cairns

To Greenwall Shelter

Appalachian Trail/Long Trail

which you can hear but cannot yet see. A few yards later, the trail crosses a footbridge over the brook.

From here the trail levels off, heading east toward the cliffs. It crosses the narrow ravine that you saw from the lookouts above and begins to head gently uphill, reaching the ice beds at 0.9 mile. A cool draft flows continually down from the boulders. The streamlet, which emerges from the base of the boulders and is the result of runoff from melting ice, is a brisk 40 degrees.

Most people who visit the ice beds like to climb on the boulders. There are many rocky perches for a picnic on a hot day.

Return by the same route.

Miles and Directions

0.0 Start at the trailhead for the Ice Beds Trail.

0.3 Pass White Rocks Overlook. View of the mountaintop and the enormous rock slide.

0.5 Pause at a scenic vista as the trail bends sharply to the right and heads downhill.

0.7 Bear left at the fork heading downhill toward a brook.

0.9 ICE BEDS! Climb the boulders to find the perfect lunch spot, then return by the same route.

1.8 Arrive back at the trailhead.

View from White Rocks Overlook.

North-Central Green Mountains

Brandon Gap to Huntington

15 Mount Horrid's Great Cliff

A short, steep hike to a cliff-top perch that rewards with long views east and west into the neighboring states of New Hampshire and New York.

General location: Goshen
Distance: 1.4 miles out and back
Approximate hiking time: 2 hours
Difficulty: Moderate
Highest elevation: 2,800 feet
Elevation gain: 620 feet

Canine compatibility: Dog friendly; no reliable water
Trail contact: Green Mountain Club, (802) 244-7037, www.greenmountainclub.org; Green Mountain National Forest, Middlebury District, (802) 388-4362, www.fs.fed.us/r9/gmfl
Map: USGS Mount Carmel (VT) Quad

Finding the trailhead: From the junction of Routes 100 and 73 in Rochester, head west on Route 73 for 9.3 miles. The trailhead parking is on the south side of the road just after the top of Brandon Gap. Cross the road to find the trailhead for the Long Trail (LT)–North. From the junction of U.S. Highway 7 and Route 73 in Brandon, head east on Route 73 for 8.2 miles. The trailhead is just before the top of Brandon Gap when approaching from this side.

The Hike

The exposed rock on Mount Horrid's Great Cliff dates back to the earliest geologic times. Though not the summit of Mount Horrid, it is truly a great cliff, towering 800 feet above Route 73 and making up the northern wall of Brandon Gap.

Although the route to the Great Cliff is via LT–North (white blazes), the trail actually heads east at first, parallel to Route 73, and then bends north into the woods at a large sign containing historical information on the LT. It is a smooth, steep climb up a boulder-strewn hillside.

At about 0.2 mile, the path passes a sign marking the boundary of the 24,237-acre Bread Loaf Wilderness Area, the largest designated wilderness within Green Mountain National Forest. The Bread Loaf Wilderness was created in 1984 and is named for Bread Loaf Mountain, which is farther north along the LT and the highest point within the wilderness area.

The trail continues to wind upward. At 0.3 mile, it mellows somewhat, though it still climbs steeply at times, quickly rising above Brandon Gap. The trail passes through stands of birches and maples, making this a colorful route during peak fall foliage.

At 0.5 mile, the ascent is aided by stone steps. The cliff becomes apparent on your right as the trail bends east. It levels off briefly, crossing some slab, where you can glimpse the opposite side of the gap through the leaves.

◀ *Mount Abraham.*

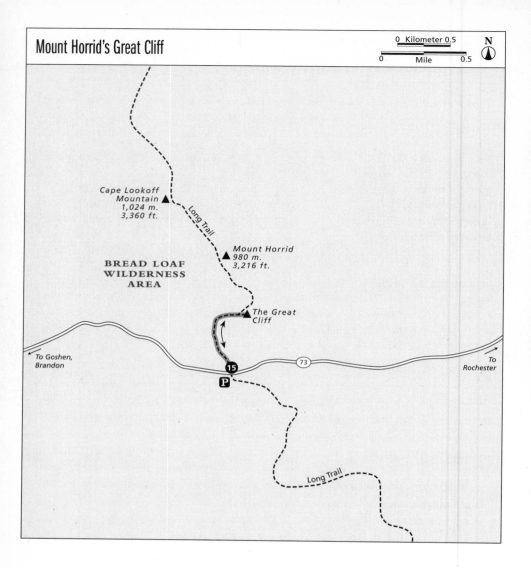

Mount Horrid's Great Cliff

Cape Lookoff
Mountain ▲
1,024 m.
3,360 ft.

Long Trail

Mount Horrid
▲ 980 m.
3,216 ft.

**BREAD LOAF
WILDERNESS
AREA**

▲ The Great
Cliff

To Goshen,
Brandon

15

P

73

To
Rochester

Long Trail

0 Kilometer 0.5

0   Mile   0.5

N

A short way later, the climb becomes steeper again and rockier, with longer stone staircases. At 0.6 mile, the steps peter out at the spur to the Great Cliff, which departs to the right (east; blue blazes). *Note:* Mount Horrid's Great Cliff is a known nesting site for peregrine falcons, typically between March and July. If falcons are nesting, the cliff area might be closed to hikers.

The short spur trail to the cliff continues to climb steadily, though less steeply at first. It levels off completely as it approaches the cliff at 0.7 mile. From this rocky outcropping, 800 feet above the road, the views extend to the Adirondacks in New York and the White Mountains in New Hampshire on a clear day.

Return by the same route.

The view west from Mount Horrid's Great Cliff.

Miles and Directions

0.0   Start at the trailhead for the LT–North.

0.2   Cross the boundary into the Bread Loaf Wilderness.

0.5   Stone steps aid the ascent.

0.6   Bear right (east) onto the spur trail to the Great Cliff.

0.7   CLIFF! Return by the same route.

1.4   Arrive back at the trailhead.

16 Silver Lake

A pristine lake with a number of tent sites and an interpretive trail with numbered historical points around its perimeter.

General location: Goshen
Distance: 5.1-mile lollipop
Approximate hiking time: 3.5 hours
Difficulty: Moderate
Highest elevation: 1,250 feet
Elevation gain: 630 feet
Canine compatibility: Dog friendly. Pets must be on a leash around the picnic area and the campground.
Trail contact: Moosalamoo Association, (802) 247-3971, www.moosalamoo.org; Green Mountain National Forest, Middlebury District, (802) 388-4362, www.fs.fed.us/r9/gmfl
Maps: USGS East Middlebury Quad

Finding the trailhead: On the east side of Lake Dunmore, follow Route 53 for 0.2 mile south of Branbury State Park. The best parking is at the main trailhead, the second lot (farther south) on the east side of the road.

The Hike

This hike is over 5 miles long, but gets a moderate rating because the elevation gain is minimal. The approach to Silver Lake is the same as the hike to Mount Moosalamoo for the first half mile, but after that it is an entirely different hiking experience, to a pristine lake rather than a mountaintop.

From the trailhead parking area, walk up a short rise to a Forest Service access road, an unpaved lane that is not opened to motorized traffic. Turn right and head up the road, which soon passes under a huge pipe, called a penstock. The penstock feeds water from Silver Lake above to a small hydroelectric power station on Route 53 below. It was built in 1922 to provide power to the iron mines in Mineville, New York, on the other side of Lake Champlain. Today, it produces electricity for over 800 homes in the Moosalamoo area. This industrial intrusion is completely hidden from hikers except for the penstock.

At 0.5 mile, the road passes the top of the Falls of Lana, an impressive waterfall fed by Sucker Brook, which is often a raging torrent. Use care if you hike down toward the falls for a better look, as the roots are slick from constant spray.

From the top of the falls, the trail parallels Sucker Brook as it climbs gently to the junction with the trail to Rattlesnake Cliffs, aka Rattlesnake Point, and the summit of Mount Moosalamoo. The junction is also notable for the public outhouse in the middle of it. Turn right, continuing along the service road.

As you climb toward the pond, ignore the various side trails and roads that enter periodically from the right. At 1.3 miles, the road reaches a grassy area at the northern tip of Silver Lake, where it meets the Rocky Point Interpretive Trail (blue blazes), the trail around the lake.

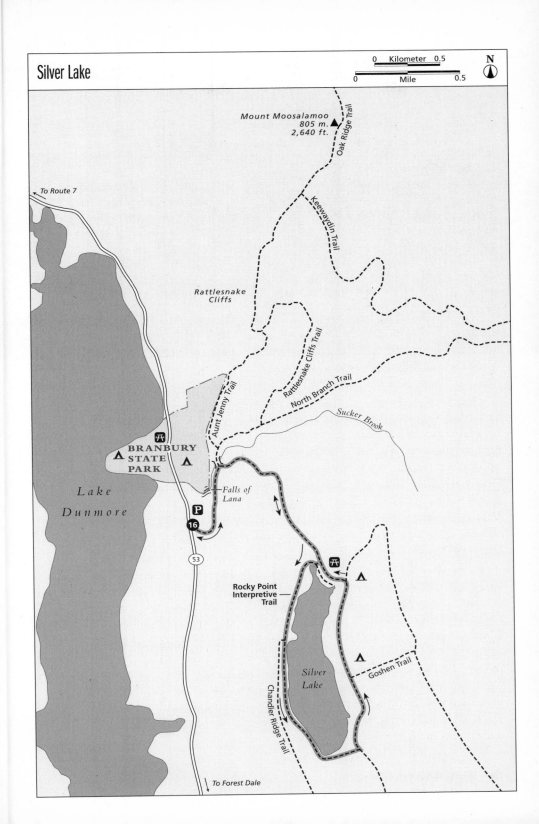

A view of Mount Moosalamoo across Silver Lake.

The 2.5-mile interpretive trail has eighteen points of interest. A booklet containing a map and an explanation of each numbered spot is available in a bin on the welcome sign. Head right, over the small dam. The dam did not create the lake—it merely enlarged it. The original lake was about 6 feet lower. It has been a backcountry destination since the mid-1800s. In its prime, from 1880 to 1910, the Silver Lake Hotel stood where the picnic area is today and entertained up to a hundred guests at a time. Now, only a few foundation stones remain.

Once past the dam, the loop trail around the lake becomes increasingly primitive, but it is well-marked. At about 1.9 miles, the Chandler Ridge Trail enters from the right. The Chandler family lived at Silver Lake for about sixty years starting in the 1870s. During that time, members of the family uncovered various tools and arrowheads left by the Abenakis. These artifacts eventually led archeologists to find two dugout canoes at the bottom of the lake, both over 600 years old.

At 2.1 miles, the trail climbs over a small cave in the rocks. Then, as you round the swampier southern end of the lake, Mount Moosalamoo dominates the view across the water.

The footing becomes drier and smoother on the second half of the lake loop. At one point, the trail passes a glade of birches leading to a piney point. The area is open under the canopy and would be a perfect place to camp, if it were allowed. Overnight camping, however, is only permitted at the designated campsite, closer to the service road.

From here the trail dips away from the lake, crosses a stream, and then rises to an intersection with the Leicester Hollow Trail at 2.8 miles, which is more forest road than footpath. A little farther, the Goshen Trail enters from the right. The path is wide, and the footing is easy. At about 3.1 miles, the path passes a number of campsites that are reserved for tent camping but have picnic tables and fire pits. Check out the old-fashioned hand-pumped drinking fountain on the left.

Just before completing the loop around the lake, the trail crosses a bridge over a flume. In 1916 the Hortonia Power Company, the predecessor to Central Vermont Public Service, built this concrete channel in order to divert water from Sucker Brook and Dutton Brook into Silver Lake and thus increase the volume of water flowing through its generators.

Complete the loop around the lake at 3.8 miles by passing through the picnic area and by the campground host's site, then retrace your steps down the service road, returning to the parking lot at 5.1 miles.

Miles and Directions

0.0 Start at the trailhead for Silver Lake and Rattlesnake Cliffs/Mount Moosalamoo.

0.5 Route to Rattlesnake Cliffs/Mount Moosalamoo departs to the left. Bear right (east), continuing up the dirt road toward Silver Lake.

1.3 LAKE! The road ends at the northern tip of Silver Lake at the Rocky Point Interpretive Trail. Bear right (west) to circumnavigate the lake.

1.9 The Chandler Ridge Trail enters from the right. Continue straight (south) on the interpretive trail next to the lake.

2.1 Pass over a small cave in the rocks.

2.8 Pass the junction with the Leicester Hollow Trail, which departs to the right.

3.1 Pass through the designated camping area on the east side of the lake.

3.8 Close the loop around the lake and retrace your steps down the dirt road.

5.1 Arrive back at the trailhead parking lot.

17 Rattlesnake Cliffs and Mount Moosalamoo

Hike to a dramatic cliff above Lake Dunmore, then through a peaceful upland forest to a modest view at the summit and a wild blueberry feast.

General location: Goshen
Distance: 6.2-mile lollipop
Approximate hiking time: 5 hours
Difficulty: Very strenuous (due to elevation gain)
Highest elevation: 2,630 feet
Elevation gain: 2,210 feet

Canine compatibility: Dog friendly. Dogs should be on leash around Rattlesnake Cliffs.
Trail contact: Moosalamoo Association, (802) 247-3971, www.moosalamoo.org; Green Mountain National Forest, Middlebury District, (802) 388-4362, www.fs.fed.us/r9/gmfl
Maps: USGS East Middlebury Quad

Finding the trailhead: On the east side of Lake Dunmore, follow Route 53 for 0.2 mile south of Branbury State Park. The best parking is at the main trailhead, the second lot (farther south) on the east side of the road.

The Hike

Moosalamoo is an Abenaki term that loosely translated means "he trails the moose" or "the moose departs." It was the original name of Lake Dunmore, then the mountain, and now the entire 22,000-acre region, which is bounded by Route 125 to the north through Middlebury Gap, Route 73 to the south, the Long Trail to the east down the main spine of the Green Mountains, and Route 53 to the west.

Mount Moosalamoo (pronounced *MOO-slah-moo*) is the highest peak in the area. It sees little foot traffic, is fairly smooth, and is not very steep above the cliffs, which makes for a pleasant walk through airy woods.

From the parking lot, walk up a short rise to a Forest Service access road, an unpaved lane that is not open to motorized traffic. Turn right, heading up the road, which soon passes under a huge pipe, called a penstock. Water from Silver Lake above travels through the penstock to a small hydroelectric power station on Route 53 below.

At 0.5 mile, the road passes the top of the Falls of Lana. The falls are named for General John Ellis Wool, an officer in the U.S. Army during the War of 1812, the Mexican–American War, and the American Civil War. General Wool came upon the Falls of Lana in 1850. *Lana* is the Spanish word for wool. Earlier, during his tour of duty in Mexico, General Wool became known as General Lana, a nickname that followed him to New England. The falls are fed by Sucker Brook, which is always dramatic and often a raging torrent. Use care if you hike down toward the falls for a better look, as the roots are slick from constant spray.

From the top of the falls, the trail parallels Sucker Brook as it climbs gently to an intersection with the trail to Silver Lake. Oddly, a public outhouse is in the center of the intersection. Turn left toward Rattlesnake Cifffs, aka Rattlesnake Point, continuing along the brook.

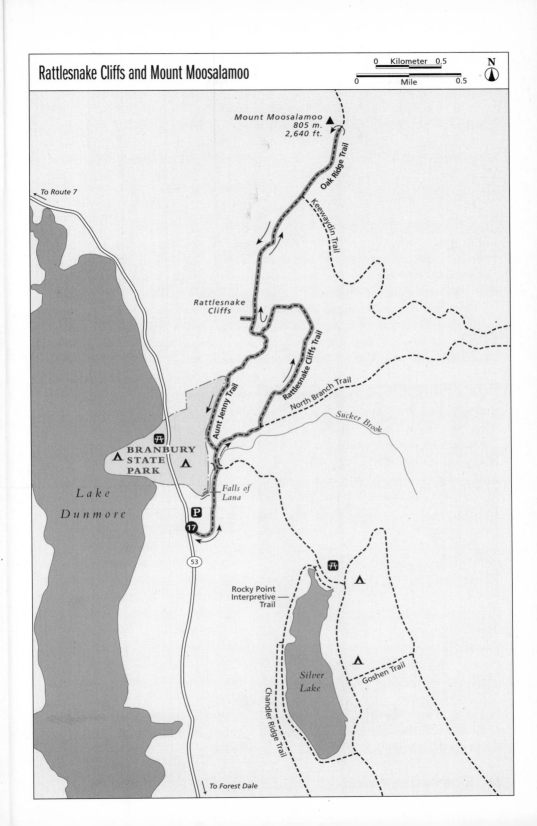

Rattlesnake Cliffs and Mount Moosalamoo

0 Kilometer 0.5
0 Mile 0.5

N

To Route 7

Mount Moosalamoo
805 m.
2,640 ft.

Oak Ridge Trail

Keewaydin Trail

Rattlesnake
Cliffs

Rattlesnake Cliffs Trail

Aunt Jenny Trail

North Branch Trail

Sucker Brook

BRANBURY
STATE
PARK

Lake
Dunmore

Falls of
Lana

17

53

P

Rocky Point
Interpretive
Trail

Silver
Lake

Chandler Ridge Trail

Goshen Trail

To Forest Dale

Soon the trail turns left again and crosses the brook via a well-constructed bridge. A primitive campsite is immediately on your right off the bridge—a nice choice if you prefer streamside camping to lake camping, which is available by Silver Lake.

Bear right at the intersection off the bridge onto the North Branch Trail. The trail is still wide here, but more like a footpath, as it leaves the stream.

At the next intersection, the Aunt Jenny Trail heads up to your left. This will be your return route. The trail is named for Jenny Rickert, who operated a tearoom near the power station in the early 1900s. Hikers often stopped there for refreshments en route to Rattlesnake Cliffs.

Continue straight for a short way, taking your next left on the Rattlesnake Cliffs Trail (blue blazes). After crossing another footbridge, the trail ascends steeply through lush temperate forest. The water bars are huge and offer the only flat steps as you climb. Eventually the trail narrows as it zigzags up the hillside, becoming less groomed. It also becomes less steep and soon crosses a stream that is often dry. It dips slightly and then traverses to the upper junction with the Aunt Jenny Trail.

From here the trail heads up again over a series of wooden steps, where you can catch glimpses of Lake Dunmore far below. A number of unofficial spurs lead to lookouts on the cliffs; however, if peregrine falcons are nesting, the cliff area will be closed from mid–March through early August. For that reason, it is best to contact the Forest Service before doing this hike if you want to be certain about visiting the cliff area.

Fireweed on Mount Moosalamoo.

At 1.5 miles, the trail reaches an intersection with the official trail to the cliff top, called Rattlesnake Point. Turn left to reach the point, which, if open, offers a spectacular view of the lake below and the mountains beyond. Rattlesnake Cliffs is a popular destination—much more popular than the summit of Mount Moosalamoo—and most hikers do not go beyond this point. To reach the summit, return to the intersection with the main trail after visiting the cliffs and continue uphill.

The trail gradually gains altitude as it continues along a spine of rock separated from the cliffs by a thin band of forest. It is tempting to stare at the lake far below through the trees, but keep an eye on the blue blazes and the trail. Grass obscures the path in places, which often seems more like a game trail than a hiking route. It is a worthwhile adventure, however. This pristine forest habitat is home to migratory songbirds and seventeen rare plant species.

As the trail climbs away from the lake, it winds through classic upland woods in a generally northern direction. Do not be surprised if you suddenly flush a grouse.

At 2.8 miles, the Keewaydin Trail enters from the right (southeast). Continue straight ahead toward the summit. The trail is now called the Oak Ridge Trail (blue blazes).

After a dozen steep rock steps, the trail passes to the right of a clearing that contains a small hut and a solar panel. The path heads around the right side of the clearing, then at 3.1 miles, breaks out on a small ledge, which is the summit. It is peppered with blueberry bushes and often moose scat. The summit of Moosalamoo is definitely an example of how the journey can be more interesting than the goal, but the view is pretty enough, primarily of nearby Sugar Hill on the next ridge to the east.

Return by the same route to the top of the Aunt Jenny Trail. Retrace the Aunt Jenny Trail to the North Branch Trail, returning to the trailhead parking lot at 6.2 miles.

Miles and Directions

0.0   Start at the trailhead for Silver Lake and Rattlesnake Cliffs/Mount Moosalamoo.

0.5   Route to Silver Lake departs to the right. Bear left (north), following the brook on North Branch Trail.

1.5   CLIFFS! Bear left on a trail that goes to the cliff area, then retrace back to the Rattlesnake Cliffs Trail to continue to the summit. (**Note:** Some trail signs and maps refer to the cliff area as "Rattlesnake Point" and others as "Rattlesnake Cliffs." It is the same place.)

2.8   The Keewaydin Trail enters from the right (southeast). Continue straight on the Oak Ridge Trail.

3.1   SUMMIT! Arrive at the summit of Mount Moosalamoo. Return by the same route to the top of the Aunt Jenny Trail.

4.3   Junction with the Aunt Jenny Trail just below Rattlesnake Point. Turn right, continuing to descend via the Aunt Jenny Trail.

5.7   Junction with the North Branch Trail. Turn right onto the North Branch Trail.

6.2   Arrive back at the trailhead.

18 Abbey Pond

A steady climb to a pristine mountain pond and a nice picnic spot on open rock by the water. Along the way, see an unusual assortment of boulders throughout the woods and a brook with many cascades and small pools. Very colorful during fall foliage season!

General location: East Middlebury
Distance: 4.2 miles out and back
Approximate hiking time: 3 hours
Difficulty: Moderate
Highest elevation: 1,700 feet
Elevation gain: 1,200 feet
Canine compatibility: Dog friendly
Trail contact: Green Mountain National Forest,
Middlebury District, (802) 388-4362, www.fs.fed.us/r9/gmfl
Maps: USGS South Mountain Quad
Special considerations: If herons are nesting on Abbey Pond, the trail may be closed. If you are planning this hike during the spring or early summer, it is worth calling ahead to see if the trail is open.

Finding the trailhead: From East Middlebury, head north on Route 116 toward Bristol for 4.2 miles. Turn right at the brown sign for the Abbey Pond Trail. The road forks immediately. Bear right and continue straight for 0.4 mile on this dirt road, which ends at the trailhead parking lot.

The shoreline of Abbey Pond.

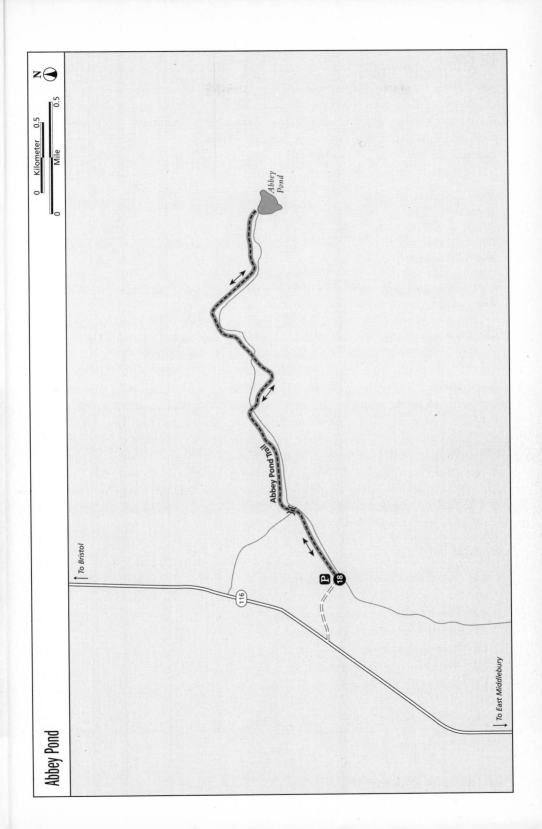

Abbey Pond

Abbey Pond Trail

116

To Bristol

To East Middlebury

P
18

N

Kilometer
0   0.5

Mile
0   0.5

The Hike

The Abbey Pond Trail (blue blazes) enters the woods on a gravel path. At first, it climbs gently, with dense hardwood forest to either side and open sky above. At about 0.1 mile, a boulder on your left grabs your attention, as it appears sliced into sections. More large boulders dot the woods. After crossing an old stone wall, the path becomes somewhat steeper and the gravel gives way to larger loose stones.

At 0.2 mile, the trail crosses a scenic brook on a solid footbridge. Cascades tumble down a small gorge on the right, then flow over smooth ledges to the left. From here the climb continues on a moderate incline on a woods road, paralleling the brook. It is a lovely setting. The trail passes by more cascades, and the surrounding woods are dotted with interesting boulders and rocky outcroppings. Large trees cling impossibly to the tops of rocks.

At 0.6 mile, the trail crosses the brook again, this time without a bridge. The driest route across the brook is toward a narrow gap between two boulders on the opposite shore.

The trail continues along the hillside and then arcs right, away from the brook, before resuming its steady climb. A few minutes later, it bends back to the left and the grade eases. The woods seem airier here than near the trailhead.

The path makes a long traverse, eventually returning to the brook. At about 1.4 miles, the trail crosses the brook by a large shallow pool. It narrows to a traditional footpath, first arcing to the left, then snaking through the woods over flat terrain.

After a long traverse to the south, the trail crosses a muddy section and arrives at Abbey Pond at 2.1 miles. There is no path around the pond, but a large rocky outcropping on the right lends itself to picnicking. The pond's shoreline is dotted with beaver dams, and Robert Frost Mountain graces the far shore. Abbey Pond is particularly pleasant during fall foliage season, when the entire shoreline turns red and orange.

Return by the same route.

Miles and Directions

0.0   Start at the trailhead for the Abbey Pond Trail.

0.1   Pass a boulder "sliced" into sections.

0.2   Cross a brook on a footbridge.

0.6   Recross the brook without a footbridge.

1.4   Cross the brook again.

2.1   POND! Return by the same route.

4.2   Arrive back at the trailhead.

19 Mount Abraham via the Long Trail

A relatively short but steady climb to an alpine summit on one of Vermont's 4,000-footers and an impressive 360-degree view.

General location: Warren
Distance: 5.2 miles out and back
Approximate hiking time: 4.5 hours
Difficulty: More challenging
Highest elevation: 4,006 feet
Elevation gain: 1,700 feet
Canine compatibility: Dog friendly, though some scrambling up rock slab on upper portion of hike. No reliable water. Dogs must be on leash in alpine zone above tree line.
Trail contact: Green Mountain Club, (802) 244-7037, www.greenmountainclub.org
Maps: USGS Lincoln Quad

Finding the trailhead: From Route 100 in Warren, take Lincoln Gap Road west toward Lincoln. This is a narrow, steep road that is closed during the winter. The trailhead is at the top of the gap. Park on either side of the road.

Just below the summit of Mount Abraham, the large white quartzite rock looks like a giant egg.

Mount Abraham via the Long Trail

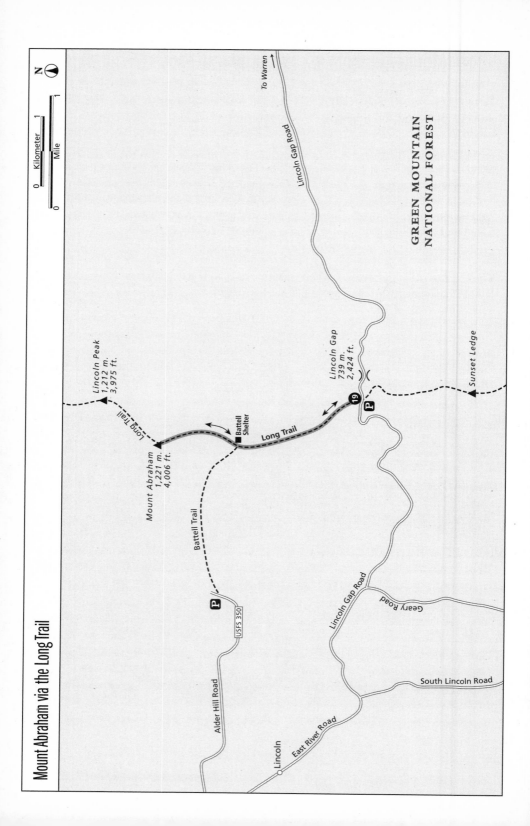

N

0 Kilometer 1
0 Mile 1

Lincoln Peak
1,212 m.
3,975 ft.

Mount Abraham
1,221 m.
4,006 ft.

Long Trail

Battell
Shelter

Long Trail

Battell Trail

Lincoln Gap
739 m.
2,424 ft.

19

P

Sunset Ledge

To Warren

Lincoln Gap Road

GREEN MOUNTAIN
NATIONAL FOREST

Lincoln Gap Road

Geary Road

South Lincoln Road

USFS 350

P

Alder Hill Road

Lincoln

East River Road

The Hike

Mount Abraham is the lowest of the five 4,000-foot peaks in Vermont. Likewise, it is the fifth-highest point in the state. It is a popular hike and relatively short for the big reward at the top, a view into three different states: New York to the west, New Hampshire to the east, and a significant portion of the spine of Vermont's Green Mountains to the north and south.

From the trailhead at Lincoln Gap, take the Long Trail (LT)–North (white blazes). The trail is flat at first and then dips through a depression as it meanders through the woods on the approach to Mount Abraham. At 0.4 mile, the trail starts to climb. It also becomes more rocky and rooted, but nothing extreme. Periodic stone steps aid your footing. The trailhead is relatively high (2,531 feet), already in the boreal zone, and the trail winds up through a typical boreal forest, primarily spruce, balsam, and birch. There are glimpses to the west through the trees.

After crossing two streams, the trail reaches the intersection with the Battell Trail, another common route up Mount Abraham, at 1.7 miles. Turn right, continuing on the LT–North to Battell Shelter at 1.8 miles. Both the trail and the shelter are named for Joseph Battell, a conservationist and former owner of the Bread Loaf Inn, who cut a trail to Mount Ellen in 1901. Battell Shelter is a simple lean-to with a picnic table. It is a convenient place to spend the night if you want to hike the entire ridge from Lincoln Gap to Appalachian Gap. The Green Mountain Club charges a small fee per person per night. Campfires are not allowed.

From Battell Shelter, turn left to continue to the summit of Mount Abraham. Soon the trees get noticeably shorter and the trail turns to slab. The ascent is steeper here, but you can catch views to the northwest between deep breaths.

Just below the summit, as the trail passes through gnarled low pines indicative of the krummholz zone at tree line, notice the large white quartzite rock on the left side of the path. It looks like a giant egg.

At 2.6 miles, the trail reaches the summit, with its 360-degree panorama. The White Mountains dominate the eastern skyline. To the west, you can see the Bristol Cliffs, Lake Champlain, and the Adirondacks in the distance. To the south, you can see down the spine of the Green Mountains as far as Killington. Mount Mansfield pokes out beyond the shoulder of Mount Ellen to the north.

The top of Mount Abraham is home to one of only three alpine zones in Vermont. The other two are on Camel's Hump and Mount Mansfield. While the alpine zone on Mount Abraham is the smallest of the three peaks, about the size of a large living room, it is home to an array of fragile alpine plants that survive despite an abbreviated two-month growing season (mid-June to mid-August). The grass on the summit is not common grass, but rare Bigelow's sedge. Be careful to step on the rocks and not the sedge.

Return by the same route.

Miles and Directions

0.0 Start at the trailhead for the LT–North.

0.4 Trail begins climbing.

1.7 Junction with the Battell Trail. Turn right, continuing on the LT–North.

1.8 Pass Battell Shelter.

2.5 Pass a large white quartzite "egg" near tree line.

2.6 SUMMIT! Return by the same route.

5.2 Arrive back at the trailhead.

LINCOLN GAP TO APPALACHIAN GAP

If you are looking for a longer hike and have two cars, it is worth hiking the entire ridge from Lincoln Gap to Appalachian Gap. This skywalk is a peak bagger's delight, crossing at least four summits—Mount Abraham (elevation 4,006 feet), Lincoln Peak (3,972 feet), Mount Ellen (4,083 feet), and General Stark Mountain (3,662 feet). Some maps also recognize Nancy Hanks Peak on the north side of Lincoln Peak and Cutts Peak on the south side of Mount Ellen, which would give you six summits in one trip. Others consider the entire ridge to be only two peaks—Lincoln and Stark—with prominent points like Mount Abraham to be part of the other two. Regardless of how you count them, this hike is one of the classic ridge walks in Vermont.

The hike is on a section of the Long Trail, commonly called the Monroe Skyline in honor of Will Monroe, who played a key role in locating it here. The total vertical gain (2,520 feet) sounds high but feels reasonable because it is spread out over 11.6 miles. Half of the climb is at the start, to the top of Mount Abraham, which makes the remaining elevation gain hardly noticeable. From the summit of Mount Abraham, the route basically follows the ridge line, rolling along to the north. That said, the mileage makes this trek formidable as a day hike for all but the fittest hikers.

If you are not up for an 11-mile day, or if you would like to combine the hike with a night in the woods, consider staying at Battell Shelter, 1.7 miles from the trailhead at Lincoln Gap, or at Dean Shelter, 1.8 miles above Appalachian Gap.

Leave one car on Route 17 at the top of Appalachian Gap, which is west of Route 100 in Waitsfield, then drive to the trailhead for Mount Abraham at the top of Lincoln Gap to begin the hike (see the Mount Abraham hike via the Long Trail).

20 Mount Abraham via the Battell Trail

A persistent ascent through four distinct climate zones to the summit of a 4,000-footer with an alpine summit that gives an expansive 360-degree view of the Adirondacks in New York, White Mountains in New Hampshire, and a large portion of the Green Mountains in Vermont.

General location: Lincoln
Distance: 5.8 miles out and back
Approximate hiking time: 5 hours
Difficulty: Very strenuous (due to elevation gain)
Highest elevation: 4,006 feet
Elevation gain: 2,500 feet

Canine compatibility: Dog friendly, though some scrambling up rock slab on upper portion of hike. No reliable water. Dogs must be on leash in alpine zone above tree line.
Trail contact: Green Mountain Club, (802) 244-7037, www.greenmountainclub.org
Maps: USGS Lincoln (VT) Quad

Finding the trailhead: From the junction of River Road and Quaker Street in Lincoln, go 0.6 mile west on Quaker Street. Turn right (east) on Alder Hill Road and go 1.3 miles. Bear right on USFS Road 350 and go another 1.0 mile. The trailhead and small parking area will be on your left.

The Hike

The Battell Trail (blue blazes) is a popular route to the top of Mount Abraham, particularly if you are on the western side of Vermont. It is named for Joseph Battell, a conservationist, Morgan horse breeder, and former owner of the Bread Loaf Inn. Battell was born in 1839 in Middlebury, Vermont, and served both in the Vermont state legislature and as a trustee of Middlebury College. Unmarried, he bequeathed several large pieces of land to Middlebury College and to the State of Vermont and is thus credited with preserving substantial tracts of forest that hikers continue to enjoy today, including Camel's Hump State Park and the John Battell Wilderness south of the Bread Loaf Wilderness. Middlebury College gradually transferred its portion of Battell's land to the USDA Forest Service between the 1930s and 1950s, which helped prompt the creation of the northern Green Mountain National Forest.

The Battell Trail is a slightly longer route to the summit of Mount Abraham than the Long Trail (LT) from Lincoln Gap, but it is interesting because it passes through four distinct climate zones, which the LT does not.

The Battell Trail begins as a smooth footpath through a hardwood forest, with ferns carpeting the sides of the path. At first, the route is a moderate stroll with some short, steep inclines. The stroll is short-lived, however. By 0.2 mile, the ascent becomes persistent, winding up the western flank of the mountain.

At 0.6 mile, the footing becomes noticeably rougher and more rooted, though the angle of ascent eases on a traverse to the south. After crossing two brooks on raised puncheon, the trail becomes smooth again, angling upward to the southeast.

Mount Abraham via the Battell Trail

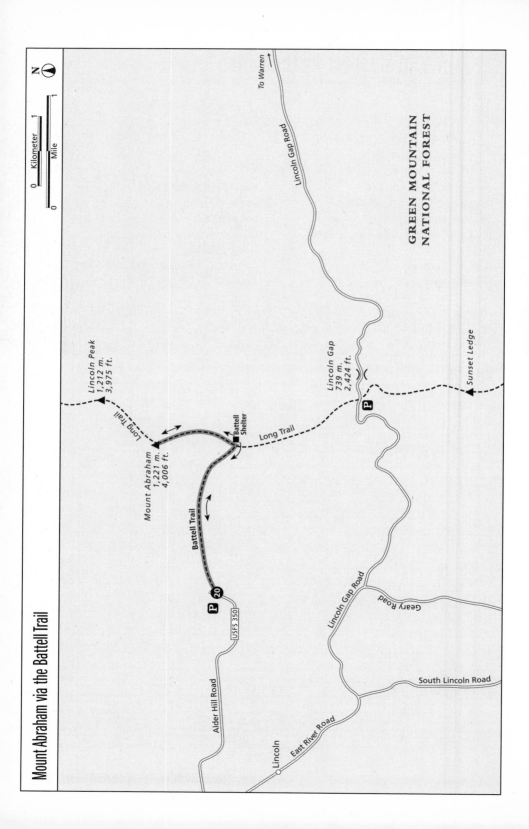

Lincoln Peak
1,212 m.
3,975 ft.

Long Trail

Mount Abraham
1,221 m.
4,006 ft.

Battell Shelter

Long Trail

Battell Trail

P
20

USFS 350

Alder Hill Road

Lincoln

East River Road

Lincoln Gap Road

Geary Road

South Lincoln Road

Lincoln Gap
739 m.
2,424 ft.

P

Sunset Ledge

GREEN MOUNTAIN
NATIONAL FOREST

Lincoln Gap Road

To Warren

N

0   Kilometer   1
0   Mile   1

Hikers departing the summit of Mount Abraham on the Battell Trail.

At 1.1 miles, the trail bends sharply to the left (north). A few minutes later, it enters the boreal zone—predominantly softwoods. Moss and rocks dot the trail, which resembles a dry streamlet. After a short while, the trail reaches a plateau and the footing improves. It continues uphill, but on a more moderate incline.

At 2.0 miles, the Battell Trail ends at the LT. Continue on the LT–North (white blazes), passing Battell Shelter a little farther up the trail. Battell Shelter is a three-sided lean-to. There is a picnic table and a nearby tent platform for use if the shelter is full. Walk along the left side of the shelter to continue to the summit.

The climb remains gentle until it reaches a series of elongated steps. From here it is a steady uphill ascent. After crossing a length of slab, a view of the summit appears ahead. With each successive piece of slab, the views become bigger, with panoramas soon opening to the south and east. The boreal forest gives way to the krummholz zone, where stunted gnarled trees grow just at tree line. After scrambling up three short "chimneys" of rock, the trail passes a huge white quartzite "egg" and then arrives at the bare summit.

The summit of Mount Abraham is in the alpine zone, typical of the arctic tundra a thousand miles to the north. It is one of only three alpine zones in Vermont. The other two are on Camel's Hump and Mount Mansfield. While the alpine zone on Mount Abraham is the smallest of the three peaks, about the size of a large living room, it is home to an array of fragile alpine plants that survive despite an abbreviated two-month growing season (mid-June to mid-August). The grass on the summit is not common grass, but rare Bigelow's sedge. Be careful to step on the rocks and not the sedge.

Return by the same route.

Miles and Directions

0.0 Start at the trailhead for the Battell Trail.

0.6 Cross two brooks on puncheon.

1.1 Bend sharply left (north) and enter boreal forest.

2.0 The Battell Trail ends at the LT. Turn left onto the LT–North.

2.1 Pass Battell Shelter.

2.9 SUMMIT! Return by the same route.

5.8 Arrive back at the trailhead.

Near Mansfield ▶

Waterbury-Stowe Area

Waterbury to Jeffersonville

21 Elephant's Head Cliff-Sterling Pond Loop

A steep ascent out of a narrow notch to a cliff-top lookout, then a moderate ascent to a scenic subalpine pond with views of Mount Mansfield along much of route.

General location: Stowe
Distance: 5.8-mile loop
Approximate hiking time: 5 hours
Difficulty: More challenging
Highest elevation: 3,100 feet
Elevation gain: 1,780 feet
Canine compatibility: Questionable due to

one ladder at the first slide crossing and some rough terrain. Only experienced hiking dogs should go on this route.
Trail contact: Green Mountain Club, (802) 244-7037, www.greenmountainclub.org
Maps: USGS Mount Mansfield Quad

Finding the trailhead: In Stowe at the junction of Routes 100 and 108, follow Route 108 (Mountain Road) north for 8.6 miles through the Stowe Mountain Resort and into Smugglers' Notch. The trailhead is on the right (north) side of the road at the Smugglers' Notch Picnic Area. From Jeffersonville, take Route 108 south for 9.4 miles. From the Stowe side, leave your car in the turnout by the gate just past the ski area and walk to the picnic area. **Note:** During the winter, Smugglers' Notch is not plowed.

The Hike

Smugglers' Notch is a deep, narrow cleft that separates the hulk of Mount Mansfield and a high ridge that includes Spruce Peak and Madonna Peak. Geologists believe the notch was formed by a river that flowed toward Stowe during the last ice age, carving the dramatic cliffs that form its walls.

The name Smugglers' Notch dates back to before the War of 1812, when the notch was used as an illegal trade route with Canada during a trade embargo with the British Commonwealth. The notch was also used during Prohibition to smuggle illegal alcoholic beverages from Canada into Vermont.

This hike takes you up the northern side of Smugglers' Notch, opposite Mount Mansfield, to the top of Elephant's Head Cliff and then to Sterling Pond via the Long Trail (LT)–North (white blazes). The LT descends to the notch road off of Mount Mansfield, follows the notch road for 0.2 mile, then reenters the woods at the south-eastern corner of the picnic area, where you should pick it up for this hike.

From the parking area, the LT passes a brown cabin. Bear left down steep ladder-like steps to the edge of the West Branch Waterbury River. The river is more like a shallow brook here. There used to be a footbridge, but it washed away during a spring flood. This is a wet crossing if the water is high. Bear left on the opposite side of the stream to continue on the LT.

The path soon crosses a smaller tributary and then bends right (south), following the stream toward Stowe. The ski trails on Mount Mansfield are visible high to your right.

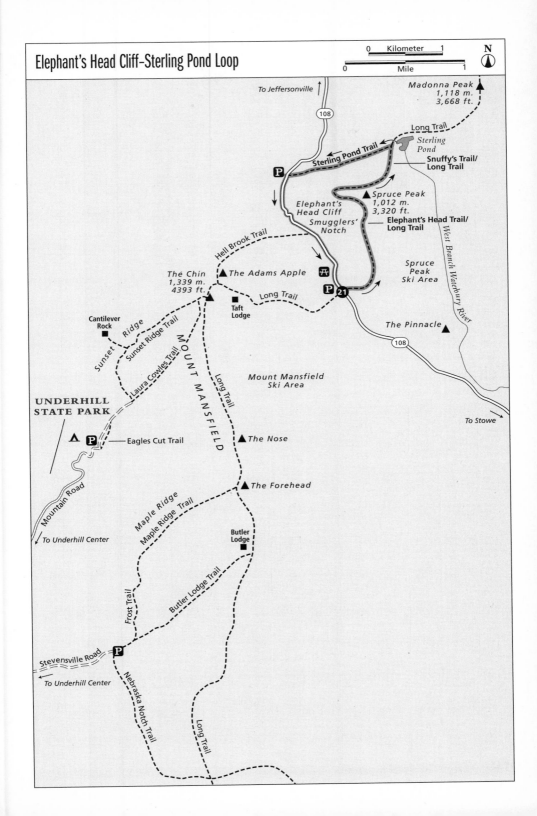

Elephant's Head Cliff-Sterling Pond Loop

To Jeffersonville ↑

0 Kilometer 1
0 Mile 1

N

Madonna Peak
1,118 m.
3,668 ft. ▲

108

Long Trail

Sterling Pond Trail ←

Sterling
Pond

P

**Snuffy's Trail/
Long Trail**

Elephant's
Head Cliff

Spruce Peak
1,012 m.
3,320 ft. ▲

Smugglers'
Notch

**Elephant's Head Trail/
Long Trail**

Spruce
Peak
Ski Area

West Branch Waterbury River

Hell Brook Trail

The Chin
1,339 m.
4393 ft. ▲

▲ The Adams Apple

🏕

The Pinnacle ▲

Long Trail

P 21

Cantilever
Rock ■

Sunset Ridge

Sunset Ridge Trail

■ Taft
Lodge

108

To Stowe →

**UNDERHILL
STATE PARK**

Laura Cowles Trail

M O U N T   M A N S F I E L D

Mount Mansfield
Ski Area

▲ P — Eagles Cut Trail

Long Trail

▲ The Nose

Mountain Road

↙ To Underhill Center

▲ The Forehead

Maple Ridge

Maple Ridge Trail

Butler
Lodge ■

Frost Trail

Butler Lodge Trail

Stevensville Road

P

← To Underhill Center

Nebraska Notch Trail

Long Trail

Hiker on the edge of frozen Sterling Pond, with a view of Madonna Peak across the pond.

The trail climbs steeply up the wall of the notch, aided by switchbacks, still heading toward Stowe. The ascent eases briefly after passing a rock wall, then begins a long traverse back to the north, still climbing persistently until it passes a rock wall on your right. The route finally mellows again as it heads back into the notch.

At 1.5 miles, the trail crosses the narrow lower portion of a landslide that dates back to 1985 and climbs a ladder. After several long switchbacks, it again crosses the slide higher up, heading south briefly. The trail then rounds another elongated switchback and continues on a long traverse back to the north.

You eventually arrive at a highly constructed staircase that climbs a large rocky knob partially buried in the mountainside. As you ascend the stairs, look across the notch for a spectacular view of Mount Mansfield and its Hell Brook cliff, a vertical rock wall on the opposite side of the notch.

The trail becomes fairly rough now as it ambles along the side of the notch wall, often hanging on the mountainside. But the climb is moderate and rewards with intermittent views, first of Camel's Hump and the top of the Mad River, then more views of Mount Mansfield.

At 2.3 miles, the trails comes to a T. Turn left (west) to take the short spur 0.1 mile to the top of Elephant's Head. (*Note:* The cliff area might be closed if peregrine falcons are nesting.) It is a steep descent to the top of the cliffs and not recommended if snow or ice are on the trail. "It's like a ski jump. There's a downward slope near the edge of the cliff," said one experienced hiker. However, if the rocks are dry, it's worth a look. From this lofty perch, the road snakes through Smugglers' Notch 1,000 feet below. Return to the junction with the LT, continuing on the LT–North.

The LT crosses a wet area, then climbs in waves, sometimes steeply, to a plateau. It winds through evergreens, which shelter the trail like walls and a roof, then bends left (northeast) and merges with a narrow ski trail, called Snuffy's Trail, at 3.0 miles. Snuffy's Trail comes from the summit of Spruce Peak (part of the Stowe Mountain Resort). This old, flat ski trail is a connector that during a good snow year allows skiers to travel between the Stowe Mountain Resort and the Smugglers' Notch Ski Area. There are unobstructed views from the ski trail into the notch and up to the "Chin" on Mount Mansfield.

At 3.3 miles, the LT comes to a junction with the Sterling Pond Trail, your way back. Bear right (northeast) to reach Sterling Pond at 3.4 miles.

Sterling Pond is a kidney-shaped tarn. It is considered a "fragile vegetation area," so stay on the trail to avoid damaging the flora. Madonna Peak, the highest point of the Smugglers' Notch ski area, and the Sterling Pond Shelter grace the opposite shoreline. There is not a specific route around the pond, though you can circumnavigate it (and a little more) by continuing on the LT to the far side, then returning via the Elephant's Head Trail back to the point where Snuffy's Trail first meets the LT (an additional 1.2 miles, not included in the total mileage in this hike description).

After enjoying the pond, retrace your steps briefly toward Elephant's Head on the Sterling Pond Trail. At 3.5 miles, where the LT/Snuffy's Trail and the Sterling Pond Trail split, bear right (west) on the Sterling Pond Trail. From here it is a steep mile down to the notch road. It is a well-used trail, wet in places and far from smooth.

At 4.5 miles, the Sterling Pond Trail ends at the notch road and an information booth. You are now on the Jeffersonville side of the notch. Turn left and follow the road back through the notch. It is a pleasant walk, even though it is by a paved road. The road is narrow and winding, with Elephant's Head and other towering cliffs on either side of you. It is especially nice to walk the notch road during the winter, when it is closed to traffic.

Close the loop at your car at 5.8 miles.

Miles and Directions

0.0 Take the LT-North from the Smugglers' Notch Picnic Area, crossing West Branch Waterbury River. Ascend the wall of the notch.

1.5 Cross an old landslide.

2.3 Spur trail to the top of Elephant's Head Cliff. Turn right to continue on the LT-North to Sterling Pond.

3.0 Merge with Snuffy's Trail, a ski trail. View of Mount Mansfield's "Chin."

3.3 Bear right (northeast) at the junction of the LT-North and the Sterling Pond Trail toward the pond.

3.4 POND! Return to junction of LT and Sterling Pond Trail.

3.5 Arrive at junction of LT and Sterling Pond Trail. Continue on Sterling Pond Trail, descending steeply to the Jeffersonville side of Smugglers' Notch.

4.5 Turn left (south) and follow the road over Smugglers' Notch.

5.8 Close the loop at the trailhead at the Smugglers' Notch Picnic Area.

HISTORY OF THE LONG TRAIL AND GREEN MOUNTAIN CLUB

The Long Trail (LT), which runs 270 miles, the entire length of Vermont from the Massachusetts border to Canada, is the original "through-trail" in North America. It was conceived in 1910 by a hiker named James P. Taylor, while waiting for the clouds to lift from the top of Stratton Mountain, though it would take another twenty years to complete. It was not a solo effort. Shortly after Taylor had the idea for the Long Trail, he gathered a group of twenty-three other passionate hikers in Burlington, Vermont. This led to the formation of the Green Mountain Club, which is credited with building the LT and which continues to maintain it today.

The LT became the model for the Appalachian Trail (AT), which was proposed eleven years later by Benton McKaye, a forester and regional planner for the USDA Forest Service, also from atop Stratton Mountain. People considering the AT from start to finish sometimes try the LT first to get a sense of through-hiking. In fact, the southern half of the LT is concurrent with the AT in Vermont.

The LT follows the high ridge of the Green Mountains, over alpine peaks, through quiet woodlands, and past pristine ponds, thus cherry-picking many of the best destinations from a hiking point of view. In addition to the LT itself, there are another 175 miles of trails that access it. Though sections of trail have changed over time due to erosion and access issues, the basic route is unchanged since it was first created.

The member-based Green Mountain Club is not only the primary steward of the LT, overseeing its maintainance, but also its advocate. In addition, the club runs programs that educate people on low-impact and other backcountry skills and publishes books and other references on the LT and its subsidiary trails. The club works with the Vermont Department of Forests, Parks and Recreation, the USDA Forest Service, the National Park Service, the Appalachian Trail Conservancy, and private landowners to ensure that day hikers and backpackers can continue to enjoy Vermont's backcountry.

22 Camel's Hump via the Monroe Trail

Eastern approach to summit of a landmark Vermont 4,000-footer where you'll find a 360-degree view from the open rock summit and rare alpine flora.

General location: Duxbury
Distance: 6.8 miles out and back
Approximate hiking time: 5.5 hours
Difficulty: More challenging
Summit elevation: 4,083 feet
Elevation gain: 1,800 feet
Canine compatibility: Dog friendly. Dogs should be on leash and on the trail (rocks) in alpine zone.
Trail contact: Vermont Department of Forests, Parks and Recreation, (802) 879-6565, www.state.vt.us/anr; Green Mountain Club, (802) 244-7037, www.greenmountainclub.org
Maps: USGS Huntington Quad

Finding the trailhead: From Route 100/Main Street in Waterbury, turn southwest on Winooski Street. Cross over the Winooski River, then turn right (northwest) on River Road toward North Duxbury. Go 4.3 miles and turn left (south) on Camel's Hump Road (no sign), which turns to dirt. At the fork, bear right following the sign reading HUMP over a bridge. At the junction of View Trail and Summit Trail, bear right following the sign for Summit Trail, which ends at the trailhead parking area.

The Hike

Camel's Hump is a Vermont landmark. Its bald summit comes to an offset point, which is visible for miles on a clear day. The mountain has had many names over the centuries. The precolonial Native Americans called it *Tawabodi-e-wadso,* or "the saddle mountain." In the early 1600s, when Samuel de Champlain first saw the mountain while exploring the region for Henry IV of France, he thought it looked like a sleeping lion and thus dubbed it *Le Lion Couchant,* or "the couching lion." In the late 1700s, Ira Allen, Ethan Allen's brother, dubbed it Camel's Rump, which was later changed to a more gentlemanly Camel's Hump.

Though one of the highlights of the Long Trail (LT) for through-hikers, the two main approaches to Camel's Hump as a day hike are not on the LT, but from the southwest via the Burrows and Forest City Trails, and from the east via the Monroe Trail. The Monroe Trail (blue blazes) is slightly longer and ascends at a moderate rate, with good footing most of the way. *Note:* Camel's Hump is a popular climb, so save this one for midweek if you can.

Enter the woods at the end of the parking area. The trail is smooth, with intermittent log water bars. It climbs gently at first through a mixed northern forest for about 0.3 mile, then ascends more purposefully, crossing several well-constructed bridges along the way. The footing remains good, though more rock strewn as you gain altitude.

Camel's Hump via the Monroe Trail

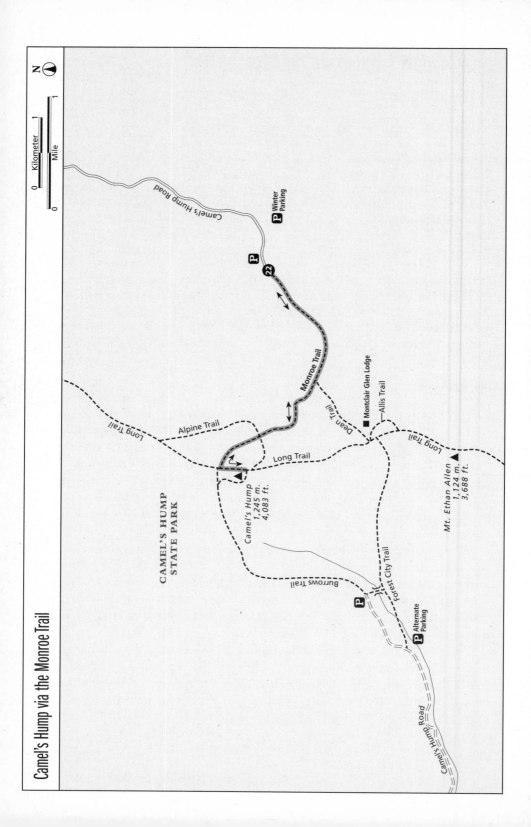

View to the south of the Monroe Skyline from the summit of Camel's Hump.

At 1.3 miles, the trail comes to the junction with the Dean Trail. Bear right (northwest), staying on the Monroe Trail. The ascent eases for a bit, then continues upward more persistently again.

At 2.0 miles, the trail crosses some rock slab, then becomes flatter and smoother until it enters softwoods. At this point, the path winds upward and becomes rocky again.

At 2.5 miles, the Monroe Trail crosses the Alpine Trail. Continue straight ahead (north) on the Monroe Trail.

At 3.1 miles, the trail comes to a clearing and another four-way junction with the Burrows Trail and the LT. The Monroe Trail ends at this junction. Turn left, following the LT–South into the alpine zone. From here it is an easy rock scramble for the last quarter mile. As you clear the tree line, look behind for views of Mount Mansfield.

The trail reaches the summit at 3.4 miles. The 360-degree view is nothing short of phenomenal. On a clear day, you can see west across the Champlain Valley to the Adirondacks, east to the White Mountains, and north and south along the high spine of the Green Mountains.

Return by the same route.

Miles and Directions

0.0 Start at the trailhead for the Monroe Trail.

1.3 Bear right (northwest) at the junction with the Dean Trail, continuing on the Monroe Trail.

2.5 Cross the Alpine Trail, continuing on the Monroe Trail.

3.1 Turn left onto the LT–South, entering the alpine zone.

3.4 SUMMIT! Return by the same route.

6.8 Arrive back at the trailhead.

Hiker on the summit of Camel's Hump with a view south of the Monroe Skyline.

23 Camel's Hump via the Forest City Trail–Burrows Trail Loop

Western loop hike over a landmark Vermont 4,000–footer, with three ledges to climb on the way up and a 360–degree panorama from the rock summit.

General location: Huntington
Distance: 5.7-mile loop
Approximate hiking time: 5 hours
Difficulty: More challenging
Highest elevation: 4,803 feet
Elevation gain: 1,950 feet
Canine compatibility: Some dogs will be challenged by the ledges on the way up. Be prepared to show proof of rabies vaccine to enter

Camel's Hump State Park if a ranger is on duty. Dogs must be on leash in the state park at the trailhead, around the Montclair Glen Lodge, and in the alpine zone around the summit.
Trail contact: Vermont Department of Forests, Parks and Recreation, (802) 879-6565, www .state.vt.us/anr; Green Mountain Club, (802) 244-7037, www.greenmountainclub.org
Maps: USGS Huntington Quad

Finding the trailhead: In Huntington Center, turn onto Taft Road. Turn onto Camel's Hump Road and follow the signs. Go past the first trailhead for the Forest City Trail. The best starting point and parking is at the upper parking lot.

The Hike

Camel's Hump is sizable in looks and in effort, but well worth the challenge. The mountain can be approached via the Long Trail (LT), but day hikers prefer to climb from either Duxbury on the eastern flank of the mountain or from Huntington on the western side. The Huntington side, described here, is about a mile shorter but arguably more challenging because of the "Stairs," a series of three consecutive ledges that require some minor scrambling. Most hikers will delight in the Stairs, which give you early views and add some topographical interest to the climb. The route described here also makes a loop, ascending via the Forest City Trail, where the Stairs are located (easier to climb up than down), and descending via the Burrows Trail. The Forest City Trail is a half-mile longer than the Burrows Trail and offers numerous views of the summit during the last third of the climb.

From the trailhead, take the short connector over a bridge to the Forest City Trail (blue blazes). At the intersection with the Forest City Trail, turn left (northeast). The sizable stream, which eventually becomes Brush Brook, will remain on your right for a while as you climb steadily through the northern hardwood forest.

Because of its distinct ecological zones that continue all the way to the summit, Camel's Hump is the site of ongoing environmental studies on the impact of acid rain and other related research. In 1965 the National Park Service named the mountain a National Natural Landmark. Research on Camel's Hump played an instrumental

Camel's Hump via the Forest City Trail–Burrows Trail Loop

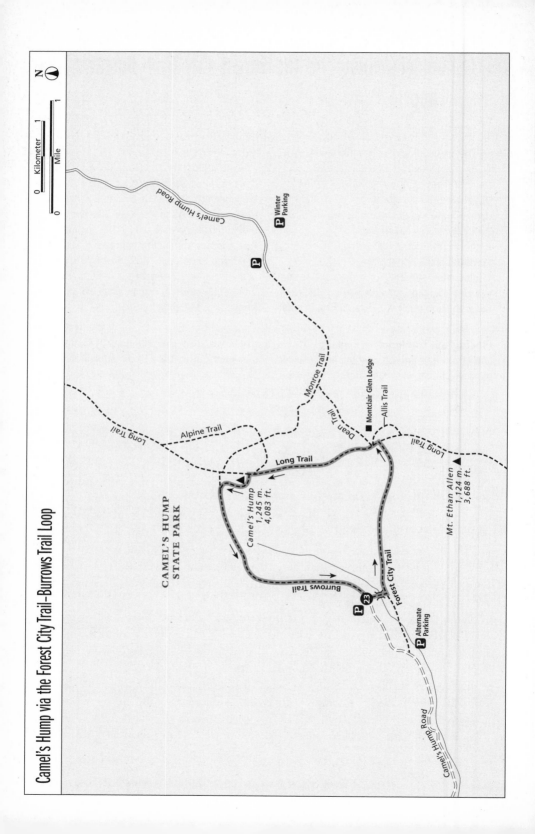

Montclair Glen Lodge on Camel's Hump.

role in linking the effects of pollutants from the Midwest to deforestation in New England, which ultimately contributed to the creation of the Clean Air Act.

At 1.5 miles, the Forest City Trail ends at a fork with the Long Trail (white blazes) to the left and the short spur to the Montclair Glen Lodge to the right. Built in 1948, the lodge is a small, cabin-like shelter typical of the LT, with plywood sleeping "shelves" and a table. The short trail to the cabin crosses a reliable brook. Space is available on a first-come, first-served basis. A Green Mountain Club backcountry caretaker, in residence from May through November, collects the per-person overnight fee.

To continue to the summit, stay on the LT–North. At 1.6 miles, the trail comes to a three-way intersection with the Dean Trail and the Allis Trail. Turn left, continuing on the LT–North. The trail now becomes noticeably steeper and rockier as you get a glimpse of the neighboring Allen Range to the right (south).

From here the trail ascends the first "stair," affording the first real view. The trail passes two enormous boulders that rest against each other to form a tunnel. Take the tunnel or walk around it to the left. From the third stair, you can see the Hump, which seems surprisingly far away.

After the stairs, the trail dips into a saddle as it approaches the summit cone. You will have frequent views of the Hump, like an imposing wall looming ahead through breaks in the low evergreen canopy.

At 2.8 miles, the LT meets the Alpine Trail, a connector to the Monroe Trail from the Duxbury side of the mountain and the summit bypass in case of bad weather. From this point, you are in the fragile alpine zone.

At 3.0 miles, the LT reaches the summit of Camel's Hump. The low flora amid the rocks is similar to rare plant life found near the Arctic Circle. A number of the slow-growing plants here are on the endangered species list and are extremely sensitive to trampling. Once on the summit, please stay on the rocks while you enjoy the endless 360-degree view.

To descend via the Burrows Trail, continue on the LT–North (do not retrace your steps). At 3.3 miles, you will reach a clearing and another three-way intersection. This is the site of a former guesthouse that was a popular destination during the Civil War; however, its popularity waned with the development of Mount Mansfield and the Stowe area. At the clearing, turn left (west) onto the Burrows Trail (blue blazes).

Descend via the Burrows Trail, closing the loop at the trailhead at 5.7 miles.

Hikers atop Camel's Hump looking south along the high spine of the Green Mountains.

Miles and Directions

0.0 Start on the connector trail, over a bridge, to the Forest City Trail.

1.5 The Forest City Trail ends at the LT. Turn left on the LT–North.

1.6 At the three-way intersection with the Dean Trail and the Allis Trail, turn left, continuing on the LT–North, climbing the three "stairs" (ledges).

2.8 Enter the alpine zone on the LT–North, continuing across the broad expanse of exposed rock.

3.0 SUMMIT! Descend by continuing on the LT–North.

3.3 Turn left (west) onto the Burrows Trail at the three-way intersection in a small clearing.

5.7 Close loop at the trailhead.

24 Mount Elmore and Balanced Rock

A popular family hike to a fire tower with a 360-degree view and then to a large boulder that seems to defy gravity.

General location: Morrisville
Distance: 5.2 miles out and back
Approximate hiking time: 4.5 hours
Difficulty: More challenging
Highest elevation: 2,608 feet
Elevation gain: 1,450 feet
Canine compatibility: Dog friendly. Dogs must have proof of current rabies vaccination to enter Elmore State Park. Dogs are not allowed at the lake area. Leash must be under 10 feet long. Do not take dogs up the fire tower.
Trail contact: Vermont Department of Forests, Parks and Recreation, (802) 476-0184, www.vtstateparks.com; Green Mountain Club, (802) 244-7037, www.greenmountainclub.org
Map: USGS Hyde Park Quad
Special considerations: A small fee is charged to enter Elmore State Park.

Finding the trailhead: From the junction of Routes 100 and 12 in Morrisville, take Route 12 south to Elmore State Park. The entrance to the park is on the west side of the road just before Lake Elmore. From the toll booth at the entrance to the state park, continue straight ahead to the trailhead. There is a cabin with a picnic table to the right in the woods near the trailhead parking area.

View of Mount Mansfield from the Mount Elmore fire tower.

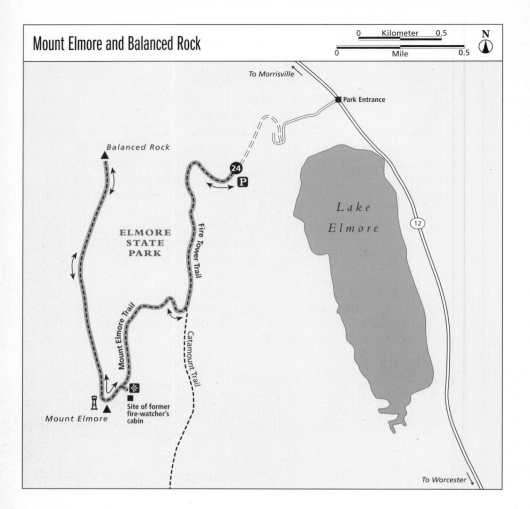

Mount Elmore and Balanced Rock

Balanced Rock

To Morrisville

Park Entrance

Lake Elmore

ELMORE STATE PARK

Fire Tower Trail

Mount Elmore Trail

Catamount Trail

Mount Elmore

Site of former fire-watcher's cabin

To Worcester

The Hike

The Worcester Range lies across the Stowe/Waterbury valley to the east of the towering Mount Mansfield ridge. Mount Elmore is the lowest peak in the Worcester Range, but also one of the more prominent and more hiked due to its position at the northern end of the range and its fire tower on top.

From the parking area, follow the Fire Tower Trail (not the Nature Trail). The route heads uphill on a fire road at first. If the gate is closed, walk around it, passing a stone chimney on the left in the woods. A few minutes later, the Beaver Pond Trail exits to the right.

At 0.5 mile, at the end of the fire road, the Catamount Trail continues straight

Balanced rock at Mount Elmore.

ahead. Take a sharp right (northwest), heading uphill on the Mount Elmore Trail (blue blazes).

The Mount Elmore Trail is a wide footpath that parallels a brook at first. The grade is fairly steep but smooth. The incline eases somewhat as the trail swings sharply right, and then continues climbing up stone steps. From here it winds up the hillside, gaining altitude in waves.

At 1.0 mile, the trail crosses small sections of wet slab before reaching the spur to a lookout on the left. The lookout is the site of the old fire watcher's cabin. The view, mainly to the east over Lake Elmore, stretches as far as Mount Washington in New Hampshire on a clear day. This is a nice destination in its own right, about halfway to the summit.

To continue to the fire tower, return to the main trail, climbing on more rugged, vertical terrain. After the short scramble, the trail levels off and arrives at a T. Turn left (south) and go just a few paces to reach the fire tower at 2.1 miles. The tower is exceptionally tall and worth the climb. The view is phenomenal considering the short hike, with Mount Mansfield dominant to the west. Jay Peak and several peaks in southern Quebec fill the northern horizon. The Presidential Range, the Franconia Ridge, and Mount Moosilauke poke up along the eastern skyline. The rest of the Worcester Range and the main spine of the Green Mountains lie to the south.

To continue to Balanced Rock, return to the T and head north, traversing the upper ridge of the mountain. The trail is flat at first and then downhill. It passes two lookouts, the first to Mount Mansfield and the second to Lake Elmore. The trail ends at Balanced Rock at 2.6 miles. As the name implies, Balanced Rock is a large boulder, about 20 feet long and 6 feet high, perched on a rock outcropping. It seems to defy gravity. Push it as hard as you like—it will not budge.

Retrace your steps back to the fire tower and then back down the Mount Elmore Trail, returning to the trailhead at 5.2 miles.

Miles and Directions

0.0   Start at the trailhead for the Fire Tower Trail, heading uphill on a fire road.

0.5   Turn sharply right at the end of the fire road onto the Mount Elmore Trail.

1.0   Pass a short spur to the site of the former fire watcher's cabin.

2.1   Turn left at the FIRE TOWER! Traverse summit ridge to north.

2.6   BALANCED ROCK! Return by the same route.

5.2   Arrive back at the trailhead.

25 Mount Hunger via the Waterbury Trail

A short, steep hike that's a favorite among locals and that ends at a spectacular bald mountaintop.

General location: Waterbury Center
Distance: 4.4 miles out and back
Approximate hiking time: 5 hours
Difficulty: Very strenuous (due to elevation gain)
Highest elevation: 3,538 feet
Elevation gain: 2,290 feet
Canine compatibility: For agile dogs only.

Inexperienced dogs, small dogs, and senior dogs will be challenged on the ledgy sections on the upper mountain.
Trail contact: Vermont Department of Forests, Parks and Recreation, (802) 879-6565, www .state.vt.us/anr; Green Mountain Club, (802) 244-7037, www.greenmountainclub.org
Maps: USGS Stowe Quad

Finding the trailhead: From Route 100 in Waterbury Center, turn east onto Howard Avenue. Turn left on Maple Street at the far end of the small village green. Turn right on Loomis Hill Road and travel up the hill approximately 2.0 miles. At the crest of the hill, the road turns to dirt and bends left, becoming Sweet Road. Continue another 1.5 miles to the parking lot and trailhead on the right (east) side of the road.

The Hike

Mount Hunger is a perennial favorite among hikers in the Stowe area because it is relatively short and has a dazzling view from its open rock summit. It is one of the primary peaks in the Worcester Range, the next ridge east of the Mount Mansfield ridge, and thus is a terrific vantage point for an unobstructed view of the entire Mansfield profile (Adams Apple, Chin, Nose, Forehead). It is also a fun hike because the upper half of the climb has many boulders and ledges to scramble up.

There are several ways to approach the summit of Mount Hunger. The Waterbury Trail (blue blazes) is both the shortest and the most vertical route. It starts out in open woods, strewn with mossy boulders. The footing is excellent, with many rock steps laid into the path by the Vermont Youth Conservation Corp. The trail climbs moderately at first, with intermittent flat sections.

There might be a number of stream crossings if the weather has been wet, but most dry up without consistent rain, except for a rocky cascade at 1.1 miles. The trail crosses the stream, then turns left, following the left bank. Over the next rise, the trail bears right across the stream between the upper and lower portion of the falls. The waterfall is often no more than a trickle, but there is always some water in the pool to the left of the crossing.

From here the trail becomes progressively rockier and steeper, though there is a brief reprieve through a patch of ferns and hobble bushes. Hobble bushes are a

Mount Hunger via the Waterbury Trail

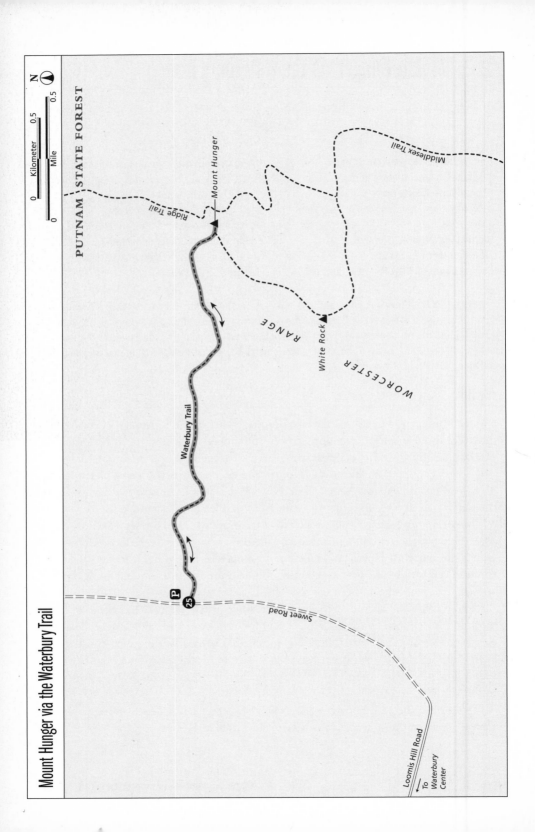

native shrub with broad leaves. They have large clusters of white flowers in midspring and then showy red berries, which are not edible, by midsummer.

The trail continues through a birch grove that was stunted during a severe ice storm in 1998, creating a break in the forest canopy. The first of several short rock walls is just around the bend. Angled cracks and narrow rock shelves provide adequate footing and handholds.

At 2.0 miles, the trail to White Rock departs to the right. From here it is a short scramble to the summit.

At 2.2 miles, the trail reaches the summit, a bare rock hump with a 360-degree view, but it is tough to take your eyes off Mount Mansfield and Camel's Hump, which dominate the skyline to the east beyond the Waterbury reservoir. The summit is treeless but is not considered

A hiker negotiating the rock on Mount Hunger.

a true alpine zone, which is generally above 4,000 feet elevation in New England. Instead, it is considered subalpine. Despite this nuance, take care to stay on the rock and off the fragile vegetation.

Return by the same route.

Miles and Directions

0.0   Start at the trailhead for the Waterbury Trail.

1.1   Cross a stream by a rocky cascade.

2.0   The trail to White Rock departs to the right.

2.2   SUMMIT! Return by the same route.

4.4   Arrive back at the trailhead.

26 Stowe Pinnacle

Short hike to an open rock knob with a 360-degree view of north-central Vermont.

General location: Stowe
Distance: 3.2 miles out and back
Approximate hiking time: 3 hours
Difficulty: More challenging
Highest elevation: 2,740 feet
Elevation gain: 1,520 feet

Canine compatibility: Dog friendly
Trail contact: Vermont Department of Forests, Parks and Recreation, (802) 879-6565, www.state.vt.us/anr; Green Mountain Club, (802) 244-7037, www.greenmountainclub.org
Maps: USGS Stowe Quad

Finding the trailhead: From the center of Stowe village, turn south onto School Street. Bear right (south) onto Stowe Hollow Road, which becomes Upper Hollow Road. The trailhead is on the left (east) side of the road, just past Pinnacle Road.

The Hike

With its impressive summit views, Stowe Pinnacle gives a huge reward for a relatively small effort. It is a favorite among Stowe locals looking for some exercise to a mountaintop destination without a full-day commitment. Located in C. C. Putnam State Forest, the Stowe Pinnacle Trail (blue blazes) is closed during mud season, April 15 to Memorial Day. Most of the hike, until the very end, is shaded, which makes it a good choice on a warm summer day.

The route begins at the back of the trailhead parking lot, traversing a meadow of wildflowers and heading directly toward the mountain. As it approaches the woods, the trail crosses a muddy area on several lengths of puncheon.

At about 0.3 mile, the trail passes a giant rock cairn on top of a small boulder. It is a tradition for all who pass to add a stone to the cairn. The trail is wide and strewn with rocks, so it is easy to find one.

After the cairn, the trail becomes fairly steep. Eventually it bends to the left and levels off, passing a sapling tepee. Then it bends back to the right and begins climbing again.

At 0.8 mile, the trail reaches a couple of switchbacks and then some muddy stone steps, a welcome aid on the sustained climb. At the top of the first series of steps, the path turns to step-like slab, then back to more real steps. This pattern continues up the steep slope until the trail reaches a height of land and a spur trail departs to the left to a lookout.

The lookout is a worthwhile spot to catch your breath. You can see the entire Mount Mansfield ridge to the west, the Waterbury reservoir and Sugarbush to the south (far left), and the village of Stowe to the north (right).

The pitch eases above the lookout. The trail bends right, descending at first, then angling upward across a rooted sidehill. It becomes steep again for a short way as it

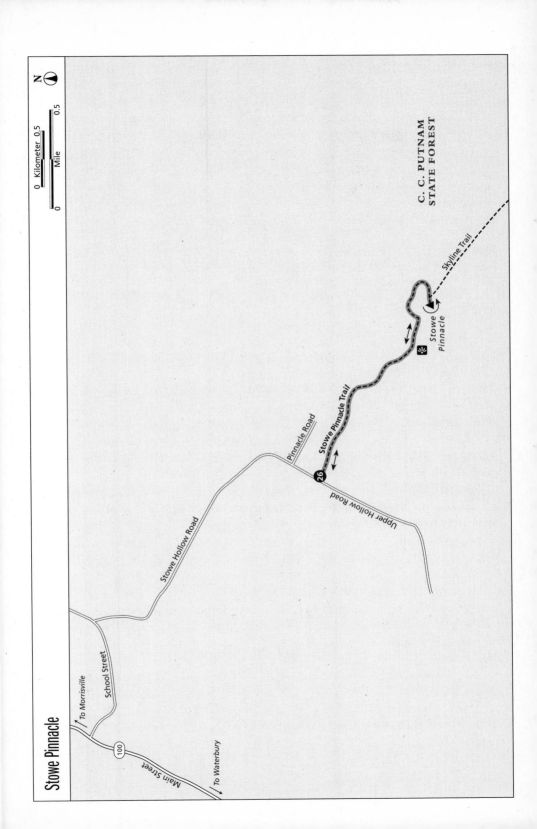

Stowe Pinnacle

circles around the north side of the summit. At 1.4 miles, the trail reaches the junction with the Skyline Trail. The Skyline Trail, which traverses the Worcester Range to Mount Hunger, departs to the left (southeast). Bear right, climbing through a pine grove, and then cross a long stretch of slab framed by scrub trees.

You then break from the trees and reach the summit at 1.6 miles. Stowe Pinnacle is accurately named. Its summit is literally a pinnacle of bedrock, giving a 360-degree view. The long views past Mount Elmore to the north, Mount Mansfield to the west, and Sugarbush to the south are impressive. The view to the east is less expansive, blocked by the wooded Worcester Range.

Return by the same route.

Miles and Directions

0.0 Start at the trailhead for the Stowe Pinnacle Trail.

0.3 Pass a giant cairn on top of a small boulder.

0.8 Climb through switchbacks and then up a series of stone steps.

1.4 Bear right at the junction with the Skyline Trail, continuing on the Stowe Pinnacle Trail.

1.6 SUMMIT! Return by the same route.

3.2 Arrive back at the trailhead.

◀ *Labs enjoying the view from Stowe Pinnacle.*

27 Mount Mansfield: The Forehead via Butler Lodge Trail– Maple Ridge Loop

Interesting climb with many ladders and rocky scrambles to the "Forehead" on Mount Mansfield's summit ridge, then a dramatic descent along an open alpine buttress on the western side of Vermont's tallest peak.

General location: Underhill Center
Distance: 6.4-mile loop
Approximate hiking time: 6 hours
Difficulty: Very strenuous (due to elevation gain)
Highest elevation: 3,940 feet
Elevation gain: 2,515 feet

Canine compatibility: Not dog friendly
Trail contact: Vermont Department of Forests, Parks and Recreation, (802) 879-6565, www .state.vt.us/anr; Green Mountain Club, (802) 244-7037, www.greenmountainclub.org
Maps: USGS Mount Mansfield Quad

Finding the trailhead: From the junction of Routes 15 and 128 in Essex Center, take Route 15 north 6.5 miles through Jericho to Underhill Flats. Turn east on River Road and go 2.7 miles to Underhill Center. At the general store in Underhill Center, bear left (northeast) on Pleasant Valley Road. Go 1.5 miles and then bear right (east) on Stevensville Road (aka Maple Leaf Road). Go another 1.0 mile to the end of the road at the trailhead parking area.

The Hike

Mount Mansfield is the tallest mountain in Vermont and among the most spectacular to hike. The profile of the 2-mile summit ridge resembles the face of a man looking skyward. The prominent points of the ridge are commonly known from south to north as the Forehead, the Nose, the Upper Lip, the Lower Lip, the Chin, and the Adams Apple. The Chin (4,393 feet) is the true summit. The loop hike described here takes you to the Forehead at the other end of the ridge. Though you will miss the chance to bag the peak, you will not feel disappointed after the invigorating scramble up ladders and ledges and the incredible views to the west during the long descent to tree line.

From the trailhead sign in the parking lot, walk up the dirt road to the left. Do not take the Nebraska Notch Trail, which is a footpath. Walk around the metal gate (not over the bridge), following the hiking trails sign. The forest road has a broad edge laden with ferns and wildflowers. After a short way, turn left (east) off the road onto the Frost Trail (blue blazes). Almost immediately, you will come to a fork. Bear right onto the Butler Lodge Trail.

The trail climbs steadily through hardwoods. At about 1.2 miles, it becomes rockier and more eroded. Rock steps aid the ascent a little higher up the slope.

At 1.6 miles, the trail reaches a short four–rung ladder up a low rock wall, though it may be easier to climb up the left side of the rock if conditions are slippery. From

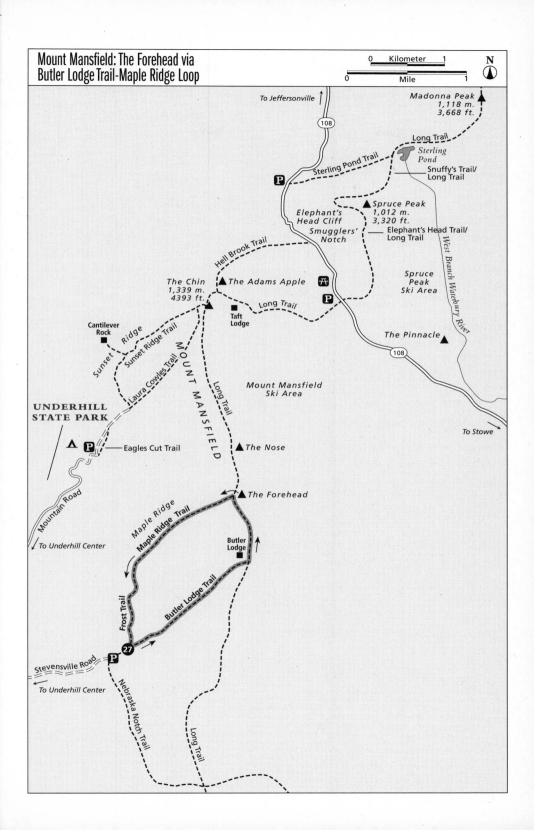

Mount Mansfield: The Forehead via Butler Lodge Trail-Maple Ridge Loop

0 Kilometer 1

0 Mile 1

N

To Jeffersonville

108

Long Trail

Madonna Peak
1,118 m.
3,668 ft.

Sterling Pond Trail

*Sterling
Pond*

Snuffy's Trail/
Long Trail

P

Elephant's
Head Cliff

▲ Spruce Peak
1,012 m.
3,320 ft.

*Smugglers'
Notch*

Elephant's Head Trail/
Long Trail

Hell Brook Trail

The Chin
1,339 m.
4393 ft.

▲ The Adams Apple

🅰

*Spruce
Peak
Ski Area*

Long Trail

P

West Branch Waterbury River

Cantilever
Rock

Sunset Ridge

Sunset Ridge Trail

■ Taft
Lodge

The Pinnacle ▲

108

Laura Cowles Trail

MOUNT MANSFIELD

*Mount Mansfield
Ski Area*

**UNDERHILL
STATE PARK**

⛺ P

Eagles Cut Trail

Long Trail

▲ The Nose

To Stowe

Mountain Road

▲ The Forehead

To Underhill Center

Maple Ridge

Maple Ridge Trail

Butler
Lodge ■

Frost Trail

Butler Lodge Trail

27 P

Stevensville Road

To Underhill Center

Nebraska Notch Trail

Long Trail

here the trail passes over more sections of slab, and the forest turns to fir trees.

At 1.8 miles, the trail passes Wallace Cutoff, arriving at Butler Lodge. Butler Lodge is a small rustic cabin typical of "lodges" on the Long Trail (LT). This one sleeps up to fourteen. There is also a water source and a privy. Space is available on a first-come, first-served basis, and a small overnight fee might be collected if a caretaker from the Green Mountain Club stops by.

From Butler Lodge, return to the junction of the Butler Lodge Trail and Wallace Cutoff. Turn left (east) on Wallace Cutoff, heading toward the LT. The path comes to another ladder, this time up a rock slab under dead tree roots. From here it winds up stone steps and then becomes smoother until the Wallace Cutoff ends at the LT.

At 1.9 miles, turn left on the LT–North (white blazes), crossing puncheon and heading upward again. The trail soon levels off, winding through the boreal forest. It heads up again over slab, squeezing between a giant glacial erratic (boulder) on the right and a wall of rock on the left, and then comes to the junction with the bad-weather bypass.

Bear left, remaining on the LT–North. The trail ascends a rock crack as it crests a hump of rock, then drops down to a third ladder. The climb gets more and more interesting as you go around and over rocks, then up yet another ladder, hanging on a rock wall. At the top of this ladder, you can see Maple Ridge ahead, which is the way down.

The trail rounds a corner, traverses a catwalk, and then scrambles up more rock. A view of Dewey Mountain and Bolton Mountain lie behind you. After climbing three more ladders, the trail enters the alpine zone. The trees shrink away, leaving wild blueberries along the slab footpath.

At 2.8 miles, the trail crests at the Forehead and the junction with the Maple Ridge Trail (blue blazes). This is the highest point of the hike, and the panorama is breathtaking. To the west, Lake Champlain glistens in the sunlight, framed by the Adirondacks on the horizon. Camel's Hump and the tall spine of the Green Mountains travel to the southern horizon. To the north and east, the hulk of Mount Mansfield looms large above you.

The Maple Ridge Trail heads back down the western side of the mountain slightly north of the route you just took up. Maple Ridge is a broad buttress, one of two open rock ridges that head down the mountain from this side. The other, Sunset Ridge, is a little farther north between the Chin and the Nose.

The descent is relatively steep until the trail reaches the junction with the Wampa-hoofus Trail, which departs to the southeast back to Butler Lodge. Continue downhill on the Maple Ridge Trail. Though still on rock slab, some side-angled, the incline becomes more moderate. Lake Champlain lies ahead the entire time.

After jumping a small gap in the rock, the trail winds around several rock outcrop-pings. Watch the blue blazes carefully in this section to stay on the trail, as it is easy to

Maple Ridge on Mount Mansfield.

get distracted by the many ledges and lookout points. Eventually the trail comes to a tall ledge, which you can descend on the right side or via a diagonal crack.

At 3.6 miles, a second trail, the Rock Garden Trail, departs to the left, also back to Butler Lodge. Bear right, continuing on the Maple Ridge Trail. The trail continues over open rock, offering long views as it descends through interesting miniature chasms and over more rock outcroppings.

At 3.9 miles, the Maple Ridge Trail comes to a junction with the Frost Trail. Turn left onto the Frost Trail. Grass and ferns begin to line the trail, and then it finally reenters the tree line. The trail turns to dirt, and white birches soon work their way into the forest mix.

There is a stream crossing just before you close the loop at 6.2 miles. Return to the trailhead at 6.4 miles.

Miles and Directions

0.0   Start by taking the dirt road to the left (not the footpath to Nebraska Notch).

0.1   Turn left (east) off the dirt road onto the Frost Trail. Immediately bear right onto the Butler Lodge Trail.

1.6   Climb the first of several ladders.

1.8   BUTLER LODGE! Take the Wallace Cutoff from the lodge toward the LT.

1.9   Turn left on the LT–North.

2.8   THE FOREHEAD! Descend via the Maple Ridge Trail along the open rock ridge.

3.6   At the junction with the Rock Garden Trail, bear right, remaining on the Maple Ridge Trail.

6.2   Close the loop at the junction with the Frost Trail near the trailhead.

6.4   Arrive back at the trailhead.

28 Mount Mansfield via the Sunset Ridge Trail

A look at gravity-defying Cantilever Rock and then an ascent to the summit of the tallest mountain in Vermont via a dramatic alpine ridge.

General location: Underhill State Park
Distance: 6.8 miles out and back (including 0.2 mile to Cantilever Rock)
Approximate hiking time: 6 hours
Difficulty: Very strenuous (due to elevation gain)
Highest elevation: 4,395 feet
Elevation gain: 2,550 feet
Canine compatibility: Dog friendly, though some challenging ledgy areas. Pets must be on leashes no longer than 10 feet in the state park campground. Proof of rabies vaccination is required to enter the state park. Puppies too young for a vaccination will not be admitted. In the alpine zone (above tree line), dogs must be on a leash no longer than 5 feet and must stay on the trail. Dogs may be off leash above the campground and below tree line.
Trail contact: Mid-May to mid-October, Underhill State Park, (802) 899-3022, or off-season, Vermont Department of Forests, Parks and Recreation, (802) 879-6565, www.vtstateparks.com; Green Mountain Club, (802) 244-7037, www.greenmountainclub.org
Maps: USGS Mount Mansfield Quad
Special considerations: There is a small day-use fee to enter the state park.

Finding the trailhead: From the junction of Routes 15 and 128 in Essex Center, take Route 15 north 6.5 miles through Jericho to Underhill Flats. Turn east onto River Road, which bends to the left and becomes Pleasant Valley Road in Underhill Center. Turn right onto Mountain Road, which ends at Underhill State Park. The trailhead is technically a mile up the dirt road from the far end of the parking lot, but this is the farthest you can drive.

The Hike

Just the fact that Mount Mansfield is the tallest peak in Vermont makes it a magnet for hikers. About 40,000 people make it to the top of this landmark each year, though they are spread out among a number of different routes along every side of the mountain. A toll road from the Stowe Mountain Resort doubles as a ski trail during the winter. It allows people to drive within a mile of the summit, giving all but the weakest hikers a chance to reach the top of this famous peak. The gondola from the ski area also brings people up to the ridge in the summertime, but it is still a demanding 2.0 miles to the summit from its highest point. The Long Trail traverses the summit ridge, allowing ascends from both the north and the south. And these are just a sampling of the ways to reach the summit of this iconic peak.

The Sunset Ridge Trail (blue blazes), one of the routes from the west, is popular because much of it is above tree line. It also has a unique side attraction called Cantilever Rock, a huge narrow boulder that extends 25 feet from a cliff parallel to the ground, seeming to defy gravity.

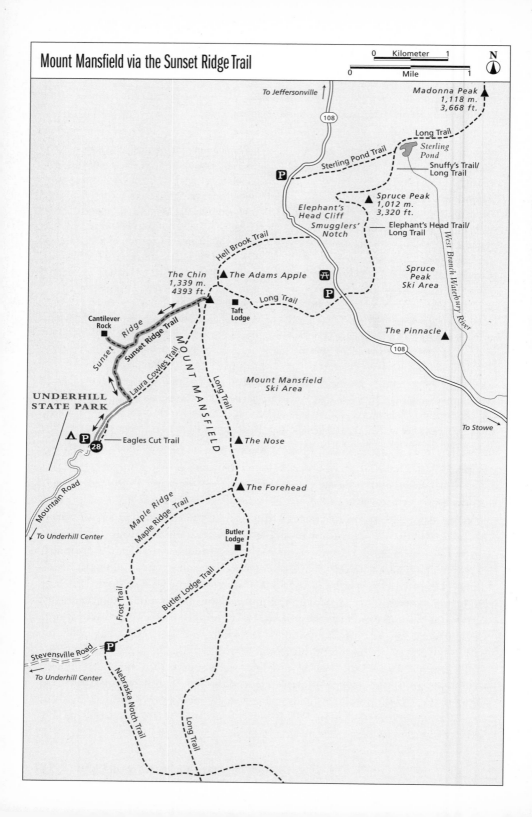

Mount Mansfield via the Sunset Ridge Trail

0 Kilometer 1

0 Mile 1

N

To Jeffersonville

Madonna Peak
1,118 m.
3,668 ft.

108

Long Trail

Sterling
Pond

Sterling Pond Trail

Snuffy's Trail/
Long Trail

Spruce Peak
1,012 m.
3,320 ft.

Elephant's
Head Cliff

Smugglers'
Notch

Elephant's Head Trail/
Long Trail

Hell Brook Trail

The Chin
1,339 m.
4393 ft.

The Adams Apple

Spruce
Peak
Ski Area

West Branch Watchury River

Cantilever
Rock

Long Trail

Taft
Lodge

Sunset Ridge

Sunset Ridge Trail

Laura Cowles Trail

The Pinnacle

108

M O U N T

Mount Mansfield
Ski Area

UNDERHILL
STATE PARK

Long Trail

To Stowe

Eagles Cut Trail

28

The Nose

M A N S F I E L D

Mountain Road

To Underhill Center

The Forehead

Maple Ridge

Maple Ridge Trail

Butler
Lodge

Frost Trail

Butler Lodge Trail

Stevensville Road

P

To Underhill Center

Nebraska Notch Trail

Long Trail

View toward The Forehead (south) from The Chin of Mount Mansfield.

The route begins in Underhill State Park in the 34,000-acre Mount Mansfield State Forest. The state park has eleven tent sites, six lean-tos, and restrooms with cold water and flush toilets, but no showers. Head up the dirt road at the end of the parking lot. The road is closed to traffic, but if you prefer a more trail-like path, take the Eagles Cut Trail (blue blazes), which starts at the upper parking lot. Both the road and the trail lead to the Sunset Ridge Trail, crisscrossing each other, until the trail merges with the road at 0.3 mile.

At 1.0 mile, the route comes to a sign-in box and the start of the Sunset Ridge Trail. Bear left into the woods and immediately cross over three bridges.

The trail comes to the lower junction with the Laura Cowles Trail at 1.1 miles. Bear left over another bridge to stay on the Sunset Ridge Trail.

After a couple more bridges, the trail starts to climb over slab, scattered rocks, and rock steps, passing over even more bridges and by a large boulder. The trail eventually comes to the first of several steeper sections of slab. From the top of it, turn around for your first view of Camel's Hump in the distance.

At 1.8 miles, the spur to Cantilever Rock departs to the left, only 0.1 mile away. It is worth the short side trip, either on the way up or on the way down. Cantilever Rock looks like a rock gangplank, protruding far into the air above a tall cliff at a 90-degree angle to the ground. Left in its seemingly impossible position when the continental glaciers receded at the end of the last ice age, Cantilever Rock continues to defy gravity, at least when viewed from below.

Return to the main trail and continue up through ferns and birches. The trail passes a chasm between three large boulders that were likely one boulder long ago. Today a streamlet flows out of the gap. A few minutes later, the trail reaches another boulder formation, this time a small cave. A streamlet flows out of the cave, too. You can walk through it, or go around on the main trail to keep your feet dry.

Several small overhangs will catch your eye as the trail winds up through the rock, then breaks out on a rocky outcropping. Technically, the alpine zone begins here. The upper Sunset Ridge and the Chin are visible above you to the left (northeast). Camel's Hump dominates the view to the right (south), and the Champlain Valley spreads out before you to the west.

Continue up the steep slab. For the rest of the route, the vistas are endless, but it is tough to take your eyes off the Chin, the distinct rocky knob that looms above. First blueberries and then wild cranberries, also called lingonberries, carpet the rocks between the scrub spruce trees.

At the sign for the Chin Natural Area, the trail bends to the right, traversing toward the Nose, and then comes to a junction with the upper end of the Laura Cowles Trail. Bear left (up).

At 3.2 miles, the Sunset Ridge Trail ends at the summit ridge, where it meets the Long Trail (LT; white blazes). Turn left onto the LT–North, crossing over puncheon and continuing toward the summit. Take care to step only on rock rather than the fragile alpine plants.

The advantage of being on the highest peak in Vermont is an expansive, unobstructed view in all directions. On a clear day, you can see all the way to Mount Royale in Montreal to the north, Whiteface Mountain and the Adirondacks across Lake Champlain to the west, Camel's Hump and the main spine of the Green Mountains to the south, and the Worcester Range (close) and the White Mountains (far) to the east.

Return by the same route.

Miles and Directions

0.0 Start walking uphill on the dirt road at the end of the parking lot or on the Eagles Cut Trail.

0.3 Eagles Cut Trail merges into the dirt road.

1.0 Bear left (north) off the dirt road onto the Sunset Ridge Trail.

1.1 Bear left at the junction with the Laura Cowles Trail, continuing on the Sunset Ridge Trail.

1.8 Turn left onto the spur to Cantilever Rock.

1.9 CANTILEVER ROCK! Retrace your steps back to the Sunset Ridge Trail.

2.0 Turn left, continuing to climb up the Sunset Ridge Trail.

3.2 Sunset Ridge Trail ends at the LT. Turn left on the LT–North.

3.4 SUMMIT! You've reached the Chin. Return by the same route.

6.8 Arrive back at the trailhead.

29 Mount Mansfield via the Long Trail-South

Steady, steep climb past Taft Lodge, with magnificent views and fun rocky scrambles on the way to the top of the tallest peak in Vermont.

General location: Smugglers' Notch
Distance: 4.6 miles out and back
Approximate hiking time: 5 hours
Difficulty: Very strenuous (due to elevation gain)
Highest elevation: 4,395 feet
Elevation gain: 2,800 feet

Canine compatibility: Not dog friendly, though experienced hiking dogs can make it. Ledges near summit are difficult for all but the most mountain-savvy dogs.
Trail contact: Green Mountain Club, (802) 244-7037, www.greenmountainclub.org
Map: USGS Mount Mansfield Quad

Finding the trailhead: From the junction of Routes 100 and 108 in the center of Stowe, turn onto Route 108 north. Go 8.1 miles through the ski area and into Smugglers' Notch. (**Note:** Route 108 through Smugglers' Notch is not open during the winter.) Park on the west side of the road in the designated parking area, then walk back 50 yards to the trailhead for the Long Trail (LT)–South.

The Hike

This hike sounds easy due to its low mileage, but don't be fooled. It climbs 2,800 vertical feet in only 2.3 miles. You should be comfortable scrambling up multiple short rock chimneys and ledgy areas before taking on this one. Save it for a dry day, as the upper part of the hike can be treacherous if the rocks are wet and the summit ridge is completely exposed to the weather. That said, the top of Mount Mansfield is the top of Vermont, with views stretching into neighboring New Hampshire, New York, and Quebec on a clear day. This route is the most popular way to hike to the summit from the Stowe side of the mountain.

Take the LT–South (white blazes) into the woods. It is a smooth climb at first through hardwoods. Soon you can hear a stream to your left through the trees. The trail ascends log steps parallel to the stream, though you cannot see it.

At 0.3 mile, the trail bends right (northwest), then climbs more steeply up big rock steps. Soon it levels off again, crossing a streamlet, then winds upward over smaller steps, gaining noticeable altitude. It sags briefly, crosses another streamlet, and then continues to climb. The trail becomes rockier with more mini–stream crossings, though many of these trickles dry up. Yellow and paper birches are noticeable throughout the forest, evidence of the higher elevation.

After more stone steps and yet another streamlet across the path, a view to the northeast teases you through the trees at 0.8 mile.

The rocky trail continues its steady climb, flattening out only on one short traverse. Though you are still under the canopy, the trees are thinning, and you can glimpse the snowmaking pond at the base of Spruce Peak.

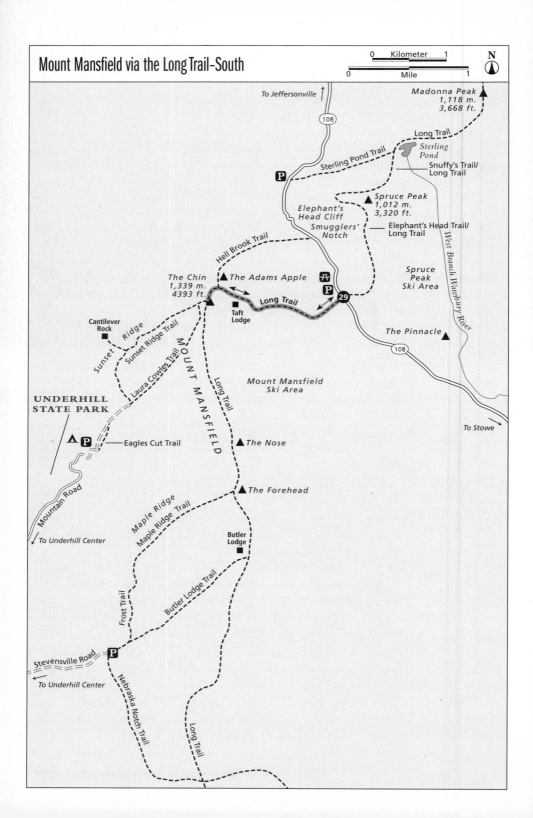

Mount Mansfield via the Long Trail-South

Kilometer

Mile

N

To Jeffersonville

108

Madonna Peak
1,118 m.
3,668 ft.

Long Trail

Sterling Pond Trail

Sterling
Pond

Snuffy's Trail/
Long Trail

P

Spruce Peak
1,012 m.
3,320 ft.

Elephant's
Head Cliff

Smugglers'
Notch

Elephant's Head Trail/
Long Trail

Hell Brook Trail

The Chin
1,339 m.
4393 ft.

The Adams Apple

Spruce
Peak
Ski Area

West Branch Waterbury River

29

Long Trail

Taft
Lodge

Cantilever
Rock

Sunset Ridge

Sunset Ridge Trail

The Pinnacle

108

M O U N T   M A N S F I E L D

Laura Cowles Trail

Long Trail

Mount Mansfield
Ski Area

UNDERHILL
STATE PARK

P

Eagles Cut Trail

Mountain Road

To Underhill Center

Maple Ridge

Maple Ridge Trail

The Nose

The Forehead

To Stowe

Butler
Lodge

Butler Lodge Trail

Frost Trail

Stevensville Road

P

To Underhill Center

Nebraska Notch Trail

Long Trail

Hikers approaching Taft Lodge on Mount Mansfield.

At 1.0 mile, the trail climbs a shallow ledge, then bends right (west) over a section of sidehill slab and up a short washout. The incline mellows as you enter a grove of hemlocks, signaling your entrance into the boreal zone. The relief is brief. The eroded trail soon winds upward and becomes rocky rubble underfoot.

After a particularly long, steep ascent up slab and ledge, you are rewarded with the first open view at 1.4 miles. Mountains trail away to the northeast from Madonna Peak on the opposite side of Smugglers' Notch. From here the trail flattens as it traverses toward the summit ridge, which towers like a wall in front of you.

At 1.6 miles, you can see the towers on top of the Forehead, one of the subpeaks of Mount Mansfield, and the famous Nosedive ski trail, which falls off a shoulder of the summit ridge like a bright green shawl.

The trail bends north, passing the junction with the Hell Brook Cutoff, which departs to the right (east). At 1.7 miles, it comes to a three-way intersection. The short left path goes to Taft Lodge, the right one goes to the lodge's outhouse, and the center path continues to the summit.

Taft Lodge sits at an elevation of 3,650 feet. The original cabin was built in 1920, then rebuilt in 1996. As with all of the cabins and shelters on the Long Trail, it is available on a first-come, first-served basis and is maintained by the Green Mountain Club. A small overnight fee may be charged. Tent camping is not allowed near the cabin.

Shortly after leaving Taft Lodge, the trail comes to the junction with the Profanity Trail, which departs to the left (west). For through-hikers on the LT, this is the summit bypass in case of bad weather. For the day hike described here, if the weather is bad, this is your turn-around point. It is dangerous to go above tree line in stormy weather.

As you near the alpine zone, the sky appears overhead as you pass through short spruce trees and alpine "grasses." You can see the ski trails and the summit ridge. After a few more steps, the Worcester Range, the next range to the east, and New Hampshire's White Mountains, on the eastern horizon, come into view.

At 2.0 miles, the trail comes to a three-way junction with the Hell Brook Trail and the Adams Apple Trail. The Adams Apple, which marks the northern end of the Mount Mansfield ridge, is the hump above you to the right. Turn left, continuing on the LT–South toward the Chin.

The trail crosses puncheon, then climbs again up open slab to a vertical rock crack. From here it is a fun scramble up another rock chimney and many ledges. The route levels off for the last 100 yards to the summit, where views of the Adirondacks (west) and White Mountains (east) will make your jaw drop.

Return by the same route.

Miles and Directions

0.0 Start at the trailhead for the LT–South.

0.3 Bend right (northwest) and climb stone steps.

1.0 Cross sidehill slab and a small washout, entering the boreal zone.

1.4 First view of Madonna Peak to the north.

1.6 View of the towers on the Forehead and the Nosedive ski trail.

1.7 TAFT LODGE! Continue on the LT–South toward the summit.

2.0 At the three-way junction with the Hell Brook Trail and the Adams Apple Trail, turn left, continuing on the LT–South.

2.3 SUMMIT! Return by the same route.

4.6 Arrive back at the trailhead.

Jay Peak ▶

Northern Green Mountains

Johnson to the Canadian Border

30 Belvidere Mountain Loop

A peaceful loop hike past a large beaver pond and Tillotson Camp to a 50-foot fire tower on one of the least traveled sections of the Long Trail.

General location: Eden Mills
Distance: 7.9-mile loop
Approximate hiking time: 6 hours
Difficulty: Very strenuous (due to elevation gain)
Highest elevation: 3,360 feet

Elevation gain: 2,140 feet
Canine compatibility: Dog friendly
Trail contact: Green Mountain Club, (802) 244-7037, www.greenmountainclub.org
Maps: USGS Eden and Hazens Notch Quads

Finding the trailhead: From Route 100 in Eden Mills, bear left on North Road, which becomes Mines Road. Go 5.1 miles to Tillotson Road. Turn left on Tillotson Road (dirt), which narrows and ends at the trailhead parking area. The trailhead is at the back left side (southwest corner) of the parking area.

Hiker at the foggy summit of Belvidere Mountain by the base of the fire tower.

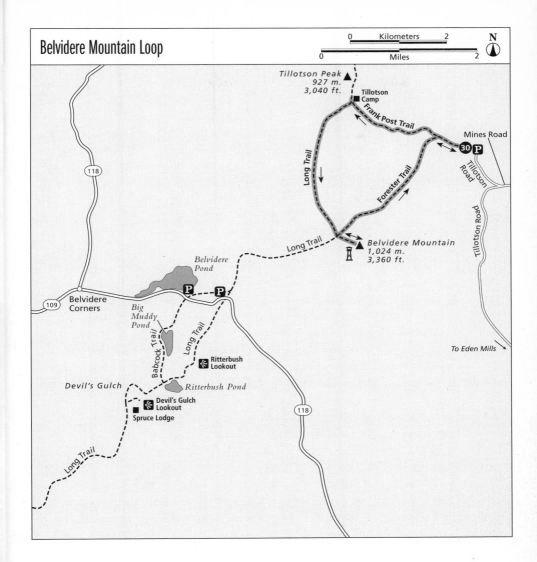

Belvidere Mountain Loop

The Hike

From the trailhead, take the Frank Post Trail (blue blazes) into the ferns and hardwoods. The trail can be wet and muddy at first, climbing gently on its approach toward the mountain.

At 0.6 mile, the trail comes to a fork, the junction with the Forester Trail. You will close the loop here on your descent. Bear right, continuing on the Frank Post Trail. The trail immediately crosses a stream and then continues its moderate, steady uphill stroll. Moose tracks and scat are common sights on the trail.

The route continues southwest, levels off for a bit, and then continues uphill again. The footing is generally smooth. At 1.4 miles, it passes a small mud pool. Above the mud pool, waist-high maple saplings encroach on the trail, cooling you as you rustle through their leaves.

At 1.6 miles, the trail becomes scattered with rocks and roots, and the softwoods become more apparent. It rounds a sharp bend to the right and then ascends a couple of switchbacks up a steeper pitch before resuming its generally northwestern course.

A short while later, the path clambers across a 4-foot rock rib with interesting swirls in the rock and a streamlet below it. The way turns steeper and more eroded as you ascend another incline, cross a streamlet, and arrive at Tillotson Camp at 2.0 miles.

Built by the Green Mountain Club in 1939, Tillotson Camp is a rustic but sturdy cabin that sleeps eight on wood "shelves" (bunks) common to cabins on the Long Trail (LT). It is available on a first-come, first-served basis. There is a nice view to the southeast from the cabin itself, with a more expansive view in the same direction from the base of a rocky outcropping through the trees on the far side of the building. This perfect picnic perch is at the base of what looks like an ancient rock slide, although it was more likely a glacial deposit.

Proceed behind the cabin to the junction with the LT (white blazes). Turn left on the LT–South, climbing past the jumble of boulders. After crossing a streamlet, the trail winds past the right side of a beaver meadow. The beaver pond is just over the next rise.

The path traverses along the southeastern side of the pond and, a few minutes later, crosses a wet plateau. It descends gently and then bends left (west) out of the mud, still on a gentle descent. Although it climbs briefly in a few spots, the long, gentle descent burns up mileage quickly.

Eventually the trails turns abruptly uphill, then eases again as it passes into the boreal forest. It levels off on a high ridge. There are no views here, but you sense the sky to either side through the trees. A few minutes later, the canopy opens overhead, but still no view as you cross another muddy plateau. Finally a view to the left (east) appears through some low trees.

The trail dips slightly and then leaves the canopy again, opening along a lawn of ferns, bunchberries, and low scrub firs at 4.4 miles.

At 4.8 miles, the trail reaches an offset four-way junction in a grassy clearing. The LT–South bends to the right. The sign reading FORESTER TRAIL AND SUMMIT points to the left, but they are not the same left. The Forester Trail, your route down, is a 90-degree left turn (northeast) about 20 yards before the turn for the tower. The short spur to the tower (blue blazes) bends more gradually to the left (east), opposite the turn for the LT–South.

At 5.0 miles, the trail comes to the fire tower. The 50-foot tower is one of only three remaining towers on the LT. The other two are on top of Glastonbury and

Ferns lining a section of the trail on Belvidere Mountain.

Stratton Mountains in the southern part of the state. This tower was built in the early 1900s and then rebuilt in the 1990s. From its viewing platform, you can see much of the spine of the Green Mountains, the Cold Hollow Mountains, and several Canadian peaks to the north. On clear days, Mount Washington in New Hampshire sits atop the eastern horizon, 71 miles away.

Even without the fire tower, the summit offers excellent views to the east. You can also see the scars of the former asbestos mine on the eastern side of the mountain, which operated from 1899 through 1993.

Return to the staggered junction with the LT and Forester Trail at 5.2 miles. Turn right onto the LT–North, then turn right again about 20 yards later onto the Forester Trail (unmarked). The Forester Trail descends steadily and the footing is generally smooth, interrupted mainly by patches of mud and moose scat.

The trail crosses a stream, then an overgrown logging road, and then another stream before coming to the junction with the Frank Post Trail at 7.3 miles, closing the loop.

Turn right (east) on the Frank Post Trail, retracing your steps for the last 0.6 mile. Arrive back at the trailhead at 7.9 miles.

Miles and Directions

0.0 Start at the trailhead for the Frank Post Trail.

0.6 Bear right at the junction with the Forester Trail, continuing on the Frank Post Trail.

2.0 TILLOTSON CAMP! Go behind the cabin and turn left on the LT–South.

4.4 Leave the forest canopy.

4.8 Take the second left onto the spur trail to the fire tower.

5.0 FIRE TOWER! Retrace back to the four-way junction with the LT and the Forester Trail. Descend via the Forester Trail.

5.2 Turn right at the junction with the LT, then right again 20 yards later onto the Forester Trail.

7.3 Close the loop at the junction with the Frank Post Trail, continuing downhill toward the trailhead.

7.9 Arrive back at the trailhead.

31 Jay Peak

Short hike on the Long Trail to the open rocky top of Vermont's northernmost ski area with stellar views into southern Quebec.

General location: Jay
Distance: 3.4 miles out and back with a loop
Approximate hiking time: 3.5 hours
Difficulty: More challenging due to elevation gain
Highest elevation: 3,861 feet
Elevation gain: 1,680 feet

Canine compatibility: Dog friendly
Trail contact: Vermont Department of Forests, Parks and Recreation, (802) 751-0110, www .state.vt.us/anr; Green Mountain Club, (802) 244-7037, www.greenmountainclub.org
Maps: USGS Jay Peak Quad

Finding the trailhead: Take Route 242 southeast of the Jay Peak ski area to a height of land known as Jay Pass. Watch for the turnout on the left (east) side of the road, which is the trailhead parking area. The trailhead is on the opposite side of the road. The Long Trail (LT) crosses the road at this point. There is no obvious sign, though you can see a small shelter on the right at the edge of the woods.

The Hike

Enter the woods on the LT–North (white blazes), immediately passing the Atlas Valley Shelter, a four-person lean-to that was built in 1967 from wood supplied by the Atlas timber company. It was not intended for overnight use, but it works in a pinch. The main trail starts out as much stream as footpath after a heavy rain, but the footing is easy. It soon begins to climb, getting increasingly steeper and becoming more rocky and well-worn.

At 0.1 mile, the LT comes to a junction with Jay Loop (blue blazes) to Jay Camp. Turn left (southwest) onto Jay Loop. Jay Camp is a cabin maintained by the Green Mountain Club, and a much better choice than the tiny Atlas Valley Shelter for those wishing to spend the night.

The path to Jay Camp is flat and wet and reaches the cabin at 0.3 mile. Constructed in 1958, it sleeps eight to twelve people and has a reliable spring about 50 feet away.

Jay Loop swings back toward the LT to the right of the cabin, rejoining it at 0.5 mile. Turn left on the LT–North, continuing toward the summit. From here the trail goes up, curves, goes up, and then curves again in a generally northwestern direction. It does not have switchbacks per se, just arcing turns.

At 0.6 mile, the softwoods start to intrude. The trail eases, winding through a berry patch. Watch the prickers along the side of the trail! The grade remains easy as the berries change to ferns and evergreens take over.

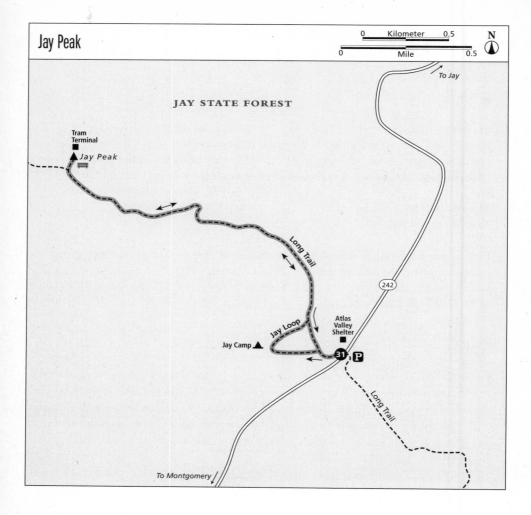

JAY STATE FOREST

Tram
Terminal
▲ Jay Peak

Long Trail

Jay Loop

Jay Camp ▲

Atlas
Valley
Shelter

242

31 P

Long Trail

To Jay

To Montgomery

At 0.9 mile, there is a break in the trees to the left, with a nice view of the neighboring peaks to the north and into Canada.

Around the next bend, the path gets steeper again, crossing short sections of slab and climbing up a number of stone steps. Nothing is extreme to this point; however, the upper part of the climb is more challenging.

Soon the spruce trees close in on the sides of the trail, which begins a longer, more sustained climb than any point so far, crossing sections of rough slab and rock. The trail makes a sharp left just below a ski trail, noticeable mainly because of the snowmaking pipes that run along the ground above the turn. After that, the slabs lengthen and can be slippery.

Stone bench near the summit of Jay Peak. ▶

At 1.6 miles, the LT meets a ski trail at the ski area boundary. Cross the ski trail, continuing on the LT, which heads up an open ridge parallel to the ski trail. The LT is more interesting. It goes over a rocky hump and then climbs steadily toward the summit cone, passing a polished stone bench just below the tram terminal at 1.8 miles.

Many hikers stop at the polished bench, away from the tourists around the tram. The bench was placed there in 2001 in memory of Dick Meunier, an employee of Jay Peak for thirty-eight years. It is inscribed with the words "A place to sit, a place to be, a place to appreciate all that we see." And there is certainly a lot to see. To the south, you can look down the spine of the Green Mountains as far as Camel's Hump. The White Mountains and the Adirondacks are visible to the southeast and southwest, respectively. To the north lies the Sutton Range in Quebec. The large lake to the northeast is Lake Memphremagog, which straddles the Canadian border.

Return by the same route, remaining on the LT–South the entire way, which is about 0.2 mile shorter than hiking around Jay Loop again. Arrive back at the trailhead at 3.4 miles.

Miles and Directions

0.0 Start on the LT-North where it crosses Route 242.

0.1 Turn left at the lower junction of the LT and Jay Loop toward Jay Camp.

0.3 JAY CAMP! Continue on Jay Loop back to the LT.

0.5 Turn left (north) at the upper junction of the LT and Jay Loop, continuing toward the summit.

0.6 Pass through a berry patch.

0.9 First view to the north through a break in the trees.

1.6 Cross a ski trail and head up a rocky ledge onto the summit ridge.

1.8 SUMMIT! Return the entire way along the LT-South.

3.4 Arrive back at the trailhead.

32 Mount Pisgah via the South Trail

A well-maintained footpath that begins with a long bridge through a sizable beaver pond and then passes a precipitous perch over Lake Willoughby en route to the top of the cliff that forms the eastern wall of Willoughby Gap.

General location: Westmore
Distance: 3.4 miles out and back
Approximate hiking time: 4 hours
Difficulty: More challenging
Highest elevation: 2,751 feet
Elevation gain: 1,450 feet
Canine compatibility: Dog friendly

Trail contact: Vermont Department of Forests, Parks and Recreation, (802) 751-0110, www .state.vt.us/anr; Westmore Trail Association, Town Clerk Office, Hilton Hill Road, Westmore 05822, (802) 525-3007
Maps: USGS Sutton Quad

Finding the trailhead: Take Route 5A north from West Burke or south from Westmore. The trailhead is just south of Lake Willoughby on the east side of the road, marked by a sign that says WILLOUGHBY STATE FOREST TRAILHEAD. The best parking is at the trailhead. Additional parking is available across the street at the trailhead for Mount Hor.

The Hike

Mount Pisgah in northern Vermont defines the eastern wall of Willoughby Gap on the eastern side of Lake Willoughby, a landlocked fjord that is both a National Natural Landmark and a designated state natural area. The lake is the centerpiece of 7,300-acre Willoughby State Forest, which was established in 1928. It is sometimes called "the Lucerne of America" for its shape and the way the mountains on either side of it rise so steeply.

Lake Willoughby is a mecca for local divers because its water is extremely clear for a lake, often with over 50 feet visibility, and because it is deep, 312 feet at its deepest point, with an average depth of 123 feet. Some of the biggest lake trout in Vermont, weighing over 30 pounds, have come out of the cold, deep waters of this lake, which is geologically unique to Vermont. It is literally a granite trough that was formed by the glaciers that covered this region during the last ice age.

Mount Pisgah offers some of the more spectacular views of the lake, but it is not a great choice if you are afraid of heights, or as a fellow hiker once stated, "I'm not scared of heights. I'm scared of edges." One perch in particular, called Pulpit Rock, provides a particularly dizzying view of the lake.

The South Trail, which is the oldest trail up the mountain, starts out tamely enough, crossing a sizable beaver pond called Swampy's Pond. The trail bends around the pond through a mixed forest of hemlock, birch, and maple, giving the area an Adirondack feel. It remains relatively flat as it winds past moss-covered boulders that seem to have been thrown at random throughout the woods.

At 0.4 mile, the trail turns left and begins climbing steadily. It remains wide, with

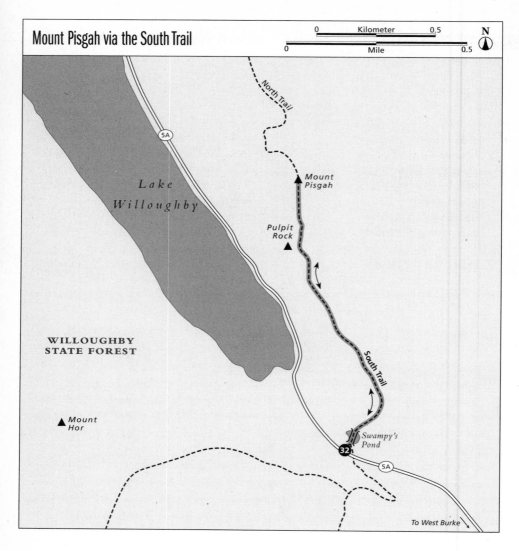

good footing, and is in excellent condition thanks to a local youth group from West-more that spends their summers on the trail crew here.

There are numerous glimpses of the lake and Mount Hor, the opposite wall of Willoughby Gap, through the trees as you ascend past rough-hewn handrails. The first clear overlook is slightly farther, over a hedge of low cedars. Watch your step—it is a big drop.

At 0.9 mile, Pulpit Rock bulges from the cliff, offering an unobstructed view of the entire lake, the cliffs to the right, Mount Hor across the gap, and a small marina 650 feet below. Use caution at every lookout, but especially this one. Stay low to get close to the edge, but still give it a lot of respect. There are no guardrails here.

The author on Pulpit Rock on Mount Pisgah.

Above Pulpit Rock, the trail bends right, away from the cliff area, and flattens out for a short stretch. Just as it begins to climb again, check out the large boulders on the right, which were actually one boulder until it broke apart. Today, it looks like a huge 3-D puzzle waiting to be put back together.

The trail climbs more moderately as it winds back toward the lake, passing through a birch grove and dipping over a single log bridge. It becomes rougher and rockier before turning away from the lake again.

At 1.7 miles, the trail climbs up a rock slab to open rock amid the scrub trees. The word TRAIL, with an arrow pointing both north and south, is painted in yellow on the rock. While technically not above tree line and not the summit, this open area is close enough and sizable enough for a summit picnic, and offers views to the south toward Burke Mountain, Newark Pond, and even the White Mountains on a clear day. The real summit is a few steps farther, unmarked, in the trees.

Return by the same route.

Miles and Directions

0.0   Start at the trailhead for the South Trail. Cross a beaver pond on a low wooden bridge.

0.4   The trail bends left (north) and begins to climb.

0.9   PULPIT ROCK! Ease your way to the edge for a view of Lake Willoughby, then continue climbing.

1.7   SUMMIT! Return by the same route.

3.4   Arrive back at the trailhead.

33 Wheeler Mountain Loop

A fun scramble over open ledges and along a cliff to a nice view of Lake Willoughby and the surrounding mountains.

General location: Barton
Distance: 4.6 miles out and back with a loop
Approximate hiking time: 4 hours
Difficulty: Moderate
Highest elevation: 2,371 feet
Elevation gain: 700 feet
Canine compatibility: Dog friendly, though

several difficult ledgy sections
Trail contact: Vermont Department of Forests, Parks and Recreation, (802) 751-0110, www .state.vt.us/anr; Westmore Trail Association, Town Clerk Office, Hilton Hill Road, Westmore 05822, (802) 525-3007
Maps: USGS Sutton Quad

Finding the trailhead: From the junction of U.S. Highway 5 and Route 5A in West Burke, go 8.3 miles north on US 5 toward Barton. Turn right (northeast) on Wheeler Mountain Road (dirt) and go 2.0 miles. The small trailhead parking area, which holds about four cars, is on the left side of the road. If the parking lot is full, please do not block the road.

The Hike

Wheeler Mountain is definitely in the category of a small hike with a big reward. Though it has a wooded summit, the journey there is mainly over open slab and traverses a dramatic cliff. This hike goes over Wheeler's summit and continues to Eagle Point, a rocky perch with a truly incredible view of the Lake Willoughby region.

The trail enters the woods on a smooth footpath that dips down to a streamlet and then heads uphill, passing along the right side of a meadow as it heads north. At 0.1 mile, at the far end of the meadow, the trail splits at the junction of the White Trail and the Red Trail. You will close the loop here at the end of the hike. Turn right (northeast) onto the Red Trail.

The Red Trail climbs easily through a mixed northern forest, then turns up steeply, arriving abruptly at the bottom of a smooth rock face. Turn left (north) at the bottom of the rock wall, over some tree roots and past scattered trillium and blueberries. The trail is more of a scramble over and up the rock here.

At 0.3 mile, there is a view to the south of the neighboring hillsides as you ascend to the first of many sections of slab. Bear right (north) up the rock, carefully following the red blazes.

The route angles up the slab to the upper junction with the White Trail at 0.4 mile. Look back for a view of Wheeler Pond. Follow the white arrows, traversing to

Hikers descending upper Wheeler Mountain by the cliff edge. ▶

A hiker enjoying the view toward Lake Willoughby from Eagle Point on Wheeler Mountain.

the east. There is still slab underfoot, though the trail enters some softwoods and soon bends to the north. From here the trail zigzags, sometimes traversing to the east and sometimes climbing to the north, in and out of the trees.

At 1.7 miles, there is a view of Burke Mountain to the southeast. The faint sporadic blazes are red and white now, and not always intuitive. The trail continues briefly toward Burke Mountain through some shrubs, then turns east again up the rock, which becomes a rock spine and then a cliff edge as you climb. At the top of the spine, a dazzling panorama awaits you. Mount Pisgah, Burke Mountain, and Bald Mountain with its fire tower are all in view.

The trail follows the cliff line through some low trees, bending to the northeast. It passes another small rock perch, then enters the woods again until it reaches the wooded summit of the mountain at 2.0 miles. From here it dips steeply and then traverses past a small cave formed by two giant boulders propped against each other.

At 2.3 miles, the trail reaches Eagle Point, a living-room–size rock perch over a 500-foot drop. Farms and forest lie below, and there is an expansive view to the east of Lake Willoughby with Mount Pisgah's tall cliffs on its far shore. Bald Mountain is to the north, set back from the lake, and Burke Mountain remains in view to the south.

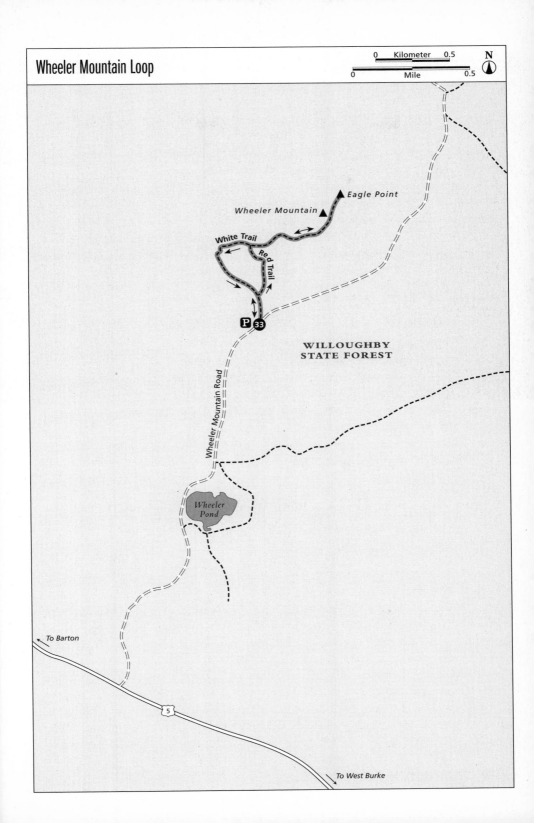

Wheeler Mountain Loop

Eagle Point

Wheeler Mountain

White Trail

Red Trail

P 33

WILLOUGHBY
STATE FOREST

Wheeler Mountain Road

Wheeler
Pond

To Barton

5

To West Burke

0   Kilometer   0.5
0   Mile   0.5

N

Return to the junction where the Red Trail and the White Trail split, at 3.5 miles. Bear right (north) on the White Trail, which continues as slab through the trees and then turns to a soft path as it heads to the west. The trail winds down the mountain on a moderate, joint-friendly grade.

At 3.7 miles, the trail goes up a small rise as it passes through the edge of an old blowdown. After passing a hillside scattered with saplings, the trail bends sharply to the left (southeast). It turns rougher on this southeastern traverse, but soon turns back west and becomes smooth again in a maple and birch forest.

At 4.2 miles, the trail crosses a streamlet. Two large metal tubs lie in the woods to the left, remnants of a maple-sugaring operation. From here the trail flattens out and becomes smooth and wide, with ferns to either side.

At 4.5 miles, the White Trail comes to the lower junction with the Red Trail at the top of the meadow, closing the loop. Continue to retrace your steps along the side of the meadow, arriving back at the trailhead at 4.6 miles.

Miles and Directions

0.0 Start by following the trail to the opposite end of a small meadow.

0.1 Turn right at the junction with the White Trail onto the Red Trail.

0.3 Ascend the first of many rock slabs. View of farmlands below.

0.4 Follow the white arrows at the junction with the White Trail. A view of Wheeler Pond is behind you.

1.7 Climb a rock spine to the edge of a cliff. Traverse the cliff edge as you climb.

2.0 SUMMIT! Continue over the wooded summit.

2.3 EAGLE POINT! Retrace the route to the upper junction of the White Trail and the Red Trail.

3.5 Bear right (north) onto the White Trail.

3.7 Pass an old blowdown.

4.2 Cross a streamlet, then pass by remnants of old maple-sugaring tubs.

4.5 Close the loop at the lower junction of the White Trail and the Red Trail. Turn right and continue along the side of the meadow.

4.6 Arrive back at the trailhead.

34 Bald Mountain (Westmore)

A long approach, then a steady climb to a grassy clearing and a tall fire tower, with commanding views into Quebec and of New Hampshire's White Mountains.

General location: Westmore
Distance: 4.0 miles out and back
Approximate hiking time: 3.5 hours
Difficulty: More challenging
Highest elevation: 3,315 feet
Elevation gain: 1,450 feet
Canine compatibility: Dog friendly
Trail contact: Vermont Department of Forests, Parks and Recreation, (802) 751-0110, www

.state.vt.us/anr; Westmore Trail Association, Town Clerk Office, Hilton Hill Road, Westmore 05822, (802) 525-3007
Maps: USGS Island Pond Quad
Special considerations: Only the very top of Bald Mountain is on state land. The rest of the hike is on private property. The owners live nearby and ask hikers to leave no trace and respect their land.

Finding the trailhead: Follow Route 5A along the shore of Lake Willoughby. In Westmore, turn east onto Long Pond Road. The trailhead and a small parking area are on the left, 0.1 mile after the boat access on Long Pond. Please do not block the gate.

The Hike

Bald Mountain in Westmore is not only the tallest Bald Mountain in Vermont, it is also the tallest peak in the Lake Willoughby area. Don't be fooled by the name: Bald Mountain in Westmore, like the other Bald Mountains in Vermont, does not have a bald summit, but it does have other redeeming features. This Bald Mountain is the only one with an elevation above 3,000 feet. It was once clear as a result of a forest fire, but gradually the flora returned. Today, the summit is a broad, grassy area with an old shelter on one side and an outstanding fire tower in the middle.

There are two approaches to the summit. The North Trail departs from Mad Brook Road. The South Trail departs from Long Pond Road and is described here because it is the easiest to find and has the best parking.

The trail begins on an old dirt logging road that is now as much grass as gravel. At the first fork, bear right. A sign on a tree says TRAIL, with an arrow underneath it pointing to the right. A short distance later, in a small clearing, the trail forks again. Bear right again at the end of the clearing. A few minutes later, the trail bends left into the woods and flattens, becoming more footpath than road, and blue blazes appear on the trees. The path traverses slightly downhill through a deciduous forest with a full canopy overhead. The many maple trees make this a colorful area during fall foliage.

At 1.0 mile, the trail crosses a streamlet, the first of several stream crossings, none of which are reliable.

After three consecutive stream crossings, the route starts to climb gently. After another small stream crossing and a series of log steps, the trail meanders through the woods on its long approach to the mountain. About ten minutes later, the uphill

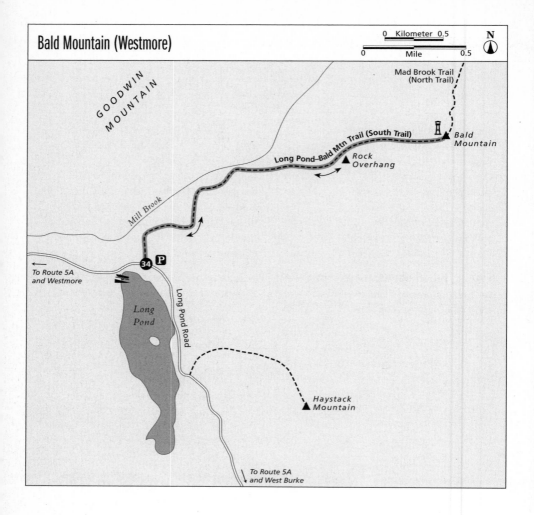

0   Kilometer   0.5

0   Mile   0.5

N

GOODWIN MOUNTAIN

Mad Brook Trail
(North Trail)

Long Pond–Bald Mtn Trail (South Trail)

Bald
Mountain

Rock
Overhang

Mill Brook

To Route 5A
and Westmore

Long
Pond

Long Pond Road

Haystack
Mountain

To Route 5A
and West Burke

climb starts in earnest, passing over a split-log bridge and then through a couple of short switchbacks before taking a more direct line up the slope. The footing remains relatively good, though more roots crisscross the trail.

At 1.7 miles, the trail bends left, passing an impressive rock overhang, 4 feet high and about 15 feet long, as if a giant wedge had been taken out of the mountainside. A root from a birch tree grows down and the trunk of another tree grows up, like two pillars in front of the shallow cave.

The trail climbs more sharply above the overhang, through a spruce grove, immediately passing an odd hole on the right. It crosses a tangle of roots and slab before

The fire tower on top of Bald Mountain. ▶

reaching a very short but hefty log bridge. The bridge crosses a narrow rock chasm, only a foot across and 6 feet deep.

From here it is a short, steady climb to the summit. The fire tower has been restored by volunteers from the NorthWoods Stewardship Center, the Northeast section of the Green Mountain Club, and the Westmore Association. The view from the tower is impressive on a clear day. To the south, Bald Hill Pond (close) and Newark Pond (farther) point toward Burke Mountain. The end of Lake Willoughby is visible to the west over the right shoulder of Haystack Mountain. Beyond Haystack, you can see Mount Pisgah and then Mount Hor on either side of Lake Willoughby. The cliffs beyond belong to Wheeler Mountain. Several peaks in Quebec lie to the north across Lake Memphremagog, and the towering Presidential Range in New Hampshire lies on the southeastern horizon.

Return by the same route.

Miles and Directions

0.0 Start on the South Trail, also called the Long Pond–Bald Mountain Trail, near Long Pond.

1.0 Cross the first of several streamlets.

1.7 Pass a small cave formed by a large rock overhang embedded in the side of the mountain.

2.0 SUMMIT! Return by the same route.

4.0 Arrive back at the trailhead.

35 Devil's Gulch-Ritterbush Pond Loop

Multifaceted loop hike that passes by two lovely ponds and includes a rocky scramble through a rock tunnel and a lush, deep ravine to a view from a high perch.

General location: Belvidere Corners
Distance: 4.6-mile loop
Approximate hiking time: 3.5 hours
Difficulty: Moderate
Highest elevation: 2,100 feet
Elevation gain: 900 feet

Canine compatibility: Dog friendly to the ponds only. Devil's Gulch is NOT dog friendly!
Trail contact: Green Mountain Club, (802) 244-7037, www.greenmountainclub.org
Maps: USGS Eden (VT) Quad

Finding the trailhead: From the junction of Routes 100 and 118 in Eden, turn north on Route 118 and go 4.7 miles. Turn right (northeast) at the sign for the Long Trail Access to find the trailhead parking.

The Hike

From the trailhead, take the Long Trail (LT)–South (white blazes) back to Route 118 and cross the road. This spot is called Eden Crossing (elevation 1,137 feet) by through-hikers on the LT. On the opposite side of the road, bear left (east) for about 25 yards along the road. At the white arrow on the tree, turn right (south) into the woods. The trail passes through a northern hardwood forest, traversing a hillside as it gently climbs.

At 0.3 mile, there is a break in the trees with a view north over Belvidere Pond below you and some surrounding wetlands. The trail rolls along a long plateau, sometimes up and sometimes down, until it leaves the height of land and begins a more sustained gentle descent.

At 1.0 mile, the path comes to a rocky outcropping. It's still under the canopy, but has a nice view of

Spruce Lodge near Devil's Gulch.

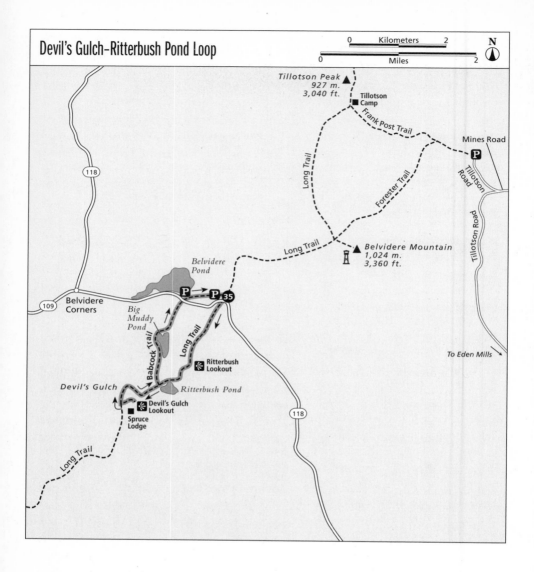

Devil's Gulch–Ritterbush Pond Loop

Kilometers

Miles

N

Tillotson Peak
927 m.
3,040 ft.

Tillotson
Camp

Frank Post Trail

Mines Road

Long Trail

Forester Trail

Tillotson Road

118

109 Belvidere
Corners

Belvidere
Pond

Belvidere Mountain
1,024 m.
3,360 ft.

Long Trail

Big
Muddy
Pond

35

Babcock Trail

Long Trail

Ritterbush
Lookout

To Eden Mills

Devil's Gulch

Ritterbush Pond

Devil's Gulch
Lookout

Spruce
Lodge

118

Long Trail

Ritterbush Pond below you to the south. From here descend rock into the woods on a steeper pitch, sometimes on stone steps, until you reach the pond. The trail levels off and then runs parallel to the western shoreline, though a distance above it, along the hillside.

At 1.7 miles, the LT comes to a junction with the Babcock Trail. Turn left (south) on the Babcock Trail, heading downhill a short way to the dirt road by the edge of the pond. Beavers have turned the saplings into stumps along this corner of the shoreline. There is an excellent view across the pond beyond a small frog pool.

Retrace your steps back to the junction. This time, turn left, continuing on the LT–South. About ten minutes later, the trail bends right up a short ladder. It then bends right again around a large rocky outcropping and heads uphill.

At 2.0 miles, a sign marks the entrance to Devil's Gulch. Two enormous disc-shaped boulders form an A-frame tunnel, a portal into the otherworldly canyon beyond. It's slow going through Devil's Gulch as you scramble over mossy rocks and marvel at the 175-foot rock walls to either side. It feels like a rain forest, with lush flora welling out of the cliffs and up from the floor of the narrow valley. Devil's Gulch is less than a quarter-mile long, but it is very memorable.

From the opposite end of the gulch, the trail heads uphill parallel to a streamlet. At 2.4 miles, it crosses the streamlet and then comes to a junction with the spur trail (blue blazes) to Spruce Lodge, a cabin maintained by the Green Mountain Club that is available on a first-come, first-served basis. Recross the stream, bearing left (east) at the sign, up stone steps toward the cabin. Due to its northern location along a less-traveled section of the LT, Spruce Lodge gives relative solitude even on weekends.

Pass the cabin and a covered picnic table, continuing on the footpath to Devil's Gulch Lookout, also called Devil's Perch on some maps. From the bench, there is a nice view over Ritterbush Pond to Belvidere Mountain. Belvidere is easy to identify due to the fire tower on its summit and the pile of asbestos tailings from an old mine on the right (east) side of the mountain.

After enjoying the view, retrace your steps back through Devil's Gulch to the junction with the Babcock Trail at 3.1 miles. This time, turn left (north) onto the Babcock Trail, heading uphill. It's a steady ascent on a rock-strewn footpath under towering maples.

At 3.4 miles, there is a break in the canopy as you reach a height of land. Here the trail becomes narrow and overgrown with lots of low-hanging vines as you approach the southern tip of Big Muddy Pond. Big Muddy Pond is long and thin, with a beaver dam at its south end. It doesn't seem very muddy when you look at it from the trail, which runs along the west side of the pond.

The trail bends right (east) around the top of the pond, then bends back north and descends steeply. At 3.9 miles, it levels off and continues through the lush forest. It reaches Route 118 at 4.2 miles at a different spot than the road crossing near the trailhead.

Cross the road and then take the Babcock Trail Extension (blue blazes) downhill. The grassy trail ends at a dirt road. Turn right (east) on the dirt road. Look for a right turn back into the woods just before you reach a parking area (the wrong one). Traverse through a pine grove, crossing a series of puncheon. From here the trail climbs gently into a mixed forest with a carpet of ferns, reaching the correct trailhead parking area at 4.6 miles.

Miles and Directions

0.0 Start by crossing Route 118 and head into the woods on the LT–South.

0.3 View of Belvidere Pond to the north. Continue on the LT–South.

1.0 View of Ritterbush Pond from a rocky outcropping. Descend toward the pond.

1.7 RITTERBUSH POND! Turn left (south) onto the Babcock Trail down to the edge of Ritterbush Pond. Return to the junction with the LT, then continue on the LT–South.

2.0 Enter Devil's Gulch through an A-frame boulder tunnel.

2.4 Turn left onto a spur trail, passing Spruce Lodge on your way to Devil's Gulch Lookout for a view of Mount Belvidere.

3.1 Return to the junction of the LT and Babcock Trail. Turn left on the Babcock Trail, heading uphill.

3.4 Approach Big Muddy Pond, then traverse above its western shoreline before descending steeply.

3.9 Traverse through a lush mixed forest.

4.2 Recross Route 118 (different spot), then take the Babcock Trail Extension, passing the wrong trailhead parking area.

4.6 Arrive back at the correct trailhead, closing the loop.

◀ *The tunnel at the entrance to Devil's Gulch.*

Appendix A: For More Information

In case of emergency, call 911, then call Green Mountain Club Headquarters, (877) 484-5053.

Trail Maintenance Organizations

Appalachian Trail Conservancy
(304) 535-6331
www.appalachiantrail.org

Green Mountain Club Headquarters and Marvin B. Gameroff Hiker Information Center
(802) 244-7037
www.greenmountainclub.org

Moosalamoo Association
(802) 247-3971
www.moosalamoo.org

Westmore Trail Association
Town Clerk Office, Hilton Hill Road, Westmore, VT 05822
(802) 525-3007

Government Agencies

Green Mountain National Forest
www.fs.fed.us/r9/gmfl
Rutland Ranger District (main office)
(802) 747-6700
Manchester Ranger District
(802) 362-2307
Middlebury Ranger District
(802) 388-4362
Rochester Ranger District
(802) 767-4261

Vermont Department of Forests, Parks and Recreation
(802) 241-3655
www.vtstateparks.com or www.state.vt.us/anr

◀ *Trout Lily.*

Appendix B: Further Reading and Resources

Guidebooks

Best Hikes with Dogs: New Hampshire & Vermont by Lisa Densmore (The Mountaineers Books, 2005).

Field Guide to North American Trees—Eastern Region by National Audubon Society (Alfred A. Knopf, 2001).

Field Guide to North American Wildflowers—Eastern Region, revised edition, by National Audubon Society (Alfred A. Knopf, 2001).

Guide to Vermont's Day Hikes by Jared Grange (Huntington Graphics, 2006).

The Long Trail End to Ender's Guide, 17th edition, by Green Mountain Club, 2007.

Long Trail Guide: Hiking Vermont's High Ridge, 26th edition, by Green Mountain Club, 2007.

Snowshoeing in Vermont: A Guide to the Best Winter Hikes by Green Mountain Club, 2005.

Maps

Vermont Atlas & Gazetteer (DeLorme)
Vermont's Long Trail End to End Map (The Wilderness Map Company)
Westmore Trail Association Map (Westmore Trail Association)

Web Sites

www.hikesafe.com
www.topozone.com

Appendix C: Hiker's Checklist

Here is a list of basic items that you should always carry in your backpack or wear whenever you venture into Vermont's backcountry:

❏ Trail map
❏ Compass
❏ Water
❏ Food
❏ Basic first-aid kit
❏ Flashlight or headlamp
❏ Pocket knife or multitool
❏ Waterproof matches or lighter
❏ Rain gear
❏ Fleece or wool top
❏ Sunscreen
❏ Lip balm
❏ Whistle
❏ Insect repellent
❏ Ball cap or other hat with a brim
❏ ID
❏ Watch
❏ Bandana
❏ Wool hat
❏ Lightweight gloves
❏ Gore-Tex or similar hiking boots with high-traction Vibram or similar soles
❏ Wool or synthetic socks
❏ Non-cotton clothing

Hike Index

About the Author

Lisa Densmore has been hiking in the Green Mountains for over thirty years. A resident of the state off and on, she went to high school at the Stratton Mountain School and then later moved back to Stratton while competing on the Women's Pro Ski Tour. She now lives on the Vermont–New Hampshire border within two hours of every trailhead and spends much of her time roaming throughout the Green Mountains as part of her work and for exercise.

Lisa Densmore on Camel's Hump.

Lisa is best known in the region as the Emmy-winning host and field producer of *Wildlife Journal* (PBS). She is also a host of *Windows to the Wild* (PBS) and various feature segments on *RSN Outdoors* (RSN). She periodically works for other networks that cover sports, adventure, and outdoor programming, such as the Outdoor Channel, VERSUS, and ESPN.

When not on-camera, Lisa is usually holding one. A passionate nature photographer, her images have appeared in such regional publications as *Vermont Life, Vermont Sports,* and *Vermont Magazine* as well as numerous national magazines. She has one of the most extensive stock photo files of Vermont's mountains, hikers, and flora. "If you can see it from a hiking trail, I've probably taken a picture of it," says Lisa. Her photographs can also be found in a number of galleries in northern New England and on her Web site, www.DensmoreDesigns.com.

Lisa complements her visual skills with writing. She has been a freelance writer since 1991 and has written hundreds of articles for almost as many magazines, including *Backpacker, Women's Running, Women in the Outdoors,* and numerous regional publications in Vermont and throughout New England.